To Auntie Iris and Uncle Alan

CW00323265

Callum
Kilburn
Christmas 2001

POETIC VOYAGES
DERBYSHIRE

Edited by Steve Twelvetree

First published in Great Britain in 2001 by
YOUNG WRITERS
Remus House,
Coltsfoot Drive,
Peterborough, PE2 9JX
Telephone (01733) 890066

HB ISBN 0 75433 344 2
SB ISBN 0 75433 345 0

FOREWORD

Young Writers was established in 1991 with the aim
to promote creative writing in children, to make
reading and writing poetry fun.

This year once again, proved to be a tremendous
success with over 88,000 entries received nationwide.

The Poetic Voyages competition has shown us the
high standard of work and effort that children are
capable of today. It is a reflection of the teaching
skills in schools, the enthusiasm and creativity they
have injected into their pupils shines clearly within
this anthology.

The task of selecting poems was therefore a difficult
one but nevertheless, an enjoyable experience. We
hope you are as pleased with the final selection in
Poetic Voyages Derbyshire as we are.

CONTENTS

Codnor CE Junior School

Joseph Shaw	53
Rebecca Stevenson	54
Adam Forster	55
Sarah Woollley	56
Jack Duncan-Handley	56
Rebecca Rawlinson	57
Cordelia Jackson	58
Emma Larkin	59

Darley Dale Primary School

Thomas Redfern	59
Ellie Fearn	60
Kelly Thorneycroft	60
Natalie Carline	61
Emma Dakin	62
James Shooter	62
Emma Allen	63
Rachel MacDonald	64
James Butler	64
Lauren Eaton	65
Luke Jackson	66
Bridie Lester	67
Sarah Renwick	68
Sean Pritty	68
✳ Callum Kilburn	69 ✳
Robert Wayne	69
Ben Twyford	70
Jenny Briddon	70
Joanne Baldock	71
Tom Dakin	71
Simon Wildgoose	72
Matthew Dutton	72
Emma Boden	73
Jenny Benyon	73
Ashley Hall	74

Furness Vale Primary School

Charlotte Harris	74
Joseph Perkins	75
Olivia Taylor	75
Kimberley Proctor	76
Melanie Schatynski	76
Stephanie Oldfield	77

Granby Junior School

Rachel Spark	77
Kimberley Statham	78
Emma-Louise Fletcher	79
Charlotte Cruise	80
Charlotte Stead	80
Laura Sloman	81
Tanya Bridget Poole	81
Fiona Stanley	82
Nichola Manaton	82
Lauren Barkes	83
Amy Doherty	83
Eleanor Hardy	84
Stephen Yau	84
Elizabeth Thornley	85
Joanne Priest	85

Grassmoor Primary School

Matthew Dart	86
Callum Milne	86
Stephanie Smith	87
Kelly Oliver	87
Rebecca Pickering	88
Amy Lawrence	89
Laura Ellis	89
Emma Hewitt	90
Claire Walker	90

Hilton Primary School

Ashley Abbey	91
Alyson Fountain	91
Rhiann Andrew	92
William Thompson	92
Callum Argyle	93
Josh Bowater	94
Alex Beech	94
Alice Autrey	95
Shaune Hill	96
Lucy Dickinson	96
Amie Broadhurst	97
Henri Dare	98
Cheryl Beech	98
Holly Frost	99
Jordan Peck	99
Bethan Jones	100
Thomas Land	100
Jack Wall	101
Greg Purnell	102
James Purnell	102
Helen Roddis	103
Genna Tooley	104
Jason Whitworth	104
Ian Richards	105
Beth Wilson	105
Carrie-Ann Hollands	106
James Wood	107
Kim Shawcross	107
Sarah Lawton	108
Emily Wheildon	108

Ilam CE Primary School

Anthony Durose	109
James Richardson	109
Hannah Tudor	110

Abigail Williams	128
Serena Jackson	129
Chloe Tidey	129
Amy Waywell	129
Joanna Tollitt	130
Alexander Fairlie	130
Alisa Hamzic	131
Byron Day	131
Rhys Jones	132
Alex Davidson	132
Lorna East	133
Sarah Eley	133
Natalie Bryan	134
Laura Blackwell	134
Laura Gilmore	135
Oliver Wilkinson	135
Josie Hough	136
Sophie Ross	136
Jake Williamson	137
Paloma Hinojosa	137
Jessica Phillips	138
Robyn Browning	138
Tom Thompson	139

Moorhead Primary School

Megan Mellor	139
Rose Akers	140
Samantha Smith	140
Charlotte Robinson	141
Simone Rochester	142
Danielle Ottewell	142
Cherrelle Barley	143
Jessica Mahey	143
Katy York	144
Holly Fowke	144
Melissa Brentnall	145

Redhill Primary School

Jessica Siddall	145
Hannah Spencer	146
Robert James Garner	146
Rosie Hunter	147
Harry Stewart	147
Grace Haspel	148
Matthew Meadows	148
Connor Hewitson	149
Becky Vesse	149
Rosanna Langworthy	150
Ellis Potter	150
Craig Seager	151
Leigh Archer	151
Susan Frankish	152
Frankie Hollingworth	152
Jade McKenzie	153
Daniel Rowling	153
Abby Mason	154
Melissa Little	154
Victoria Richardson	155
Alex Smith	155
James Elcock	156
Thomas Mills	156
Anna Perkins	157
Laura Barber	157
Elliot Emery	158
Emma Little	158
James Lapping	159
Abigail Teflise	159
James McKinnon	160
Luke Spinks	160
Josh Woods	160
Amy Davies	161
Hattie Owens	161
Jessica Smyth	161
Robert Howarth	162
Benjamin Harrison	162

Natasha Brough	180
Lexy Else	181
Charlotte Day	181

St Werburgh's Primary School, Spondon

Carly Howard	182
Andrew Marriott	182
Abigail Knapp	183
Jessica Langton	184
Sarah Broomfield	185
Emily Langton	186
Charlotte Rodgers	186
Nicol Winfield	187
Jessica Gallagher	188
Emma Shore	188
Alice Williamson	189
Daniel Metcalf	190
Sean Shields	190
Josie Hardaker	191
Bradley Larimore	192
Becky Cussens	192
Cher Maxwell	193
Christina Ford	193
Paris Sullivan	194
Shannon Smith	194
Keylie Banyard	195
Dominic Hill	196
Louis Danvers	196
Natasha Waring	197
Amy Milwain	198
Grant James Ellis	199
Lucy D'Amico	199
Jordan Trewhella	200
Georgia Hardaker	200
Lucy Siena	201
Charlie Lawson	201

The Poems

SLEEP IS NOT ALL THAT IT SEEMS - MON VOYAGE

I'm on my own journey
In my own mind
Trying to leave
The whole world behind

Thoughts buzz through my head
I wonder what to do
I'm on a creamy cloud
Reading a book or two

I'm swimming through an ocean,
Flying through the sky
Trying to keep up OK
Following the distant cry

I'm coming to the end
Of one of my beautiful dreams
Coming back to my world
Sleep is not all as it seems.

Cecelia Broadbent (9)
Ashbourne PNEU School

MY FUTURE JOURNEY

On the plane past the Atlantic sea,
I wonder what the future holds for me?
It fills my head with golden glee,
As I look in the marble sea
I see my reflection
Looking back at me.

Oliver Glover (9)
Ashbourne PNEU School

DREAMS

As I fell asleep
The stars outside
Picked me up and
Threw me far into the sky.

I was falling onto a crusty wooden ship
That floated on a blue and green seadrift.
No steam, no working machines,
I only heard the heaving of strong men,
Setting their lines, singing in their worthy minds,
Pleading for freedom for their backs behind as the shore appeared,
I saw the castle standing clear,
The moss growing lofty.
I heard hands clapping and three cheers,
The sailors had returned from so many years
They had been away,
As the king started to say
And then a hand slapped me, it was morning.

Hannah Wilson (9)
Ashbourne PNEU School

ON THE AEROPLANE

I sat on the aeroplane playing the most fantastic game,
First there was a bumpety bump, then there came a great big thump.
The seats were very close together, the journey seemed to take forever.
Then I saw something black, it looked like a big fat cat,
It was only a little bird, but then came a great big herd
Of big fat flapping birds, then they dived at my food,
I thought it was very rude.
I shut the flap and then there was a splat, splat, splat!

George Benton (8)
Ashbourne PNEU School

I AM GOING TO THE SHOPS

I am going to the shops.
Why?
To get some ice cream.
Why?
Because you ate the last lot.
Why?
Because you were hungry.
Why?
Because I wouldn't let you have anything the day before.
Why?
Because you wouldn't tidy your room.
Why?
Can't you stop saying why?
Why?
I don't know what's come over you, but you must have why disease.
What?

Alex Harman (8)
Bamford Primary School

CALL A TORTOISE SLOWCOACH!

Call a tortoise slowcoach,
Call a tortoise race loser,
Call a tortoise shell face,
Call a tortoise ugly shell,
Call a tortoise little legs,
Call a tortoise heavy back.

Anne-Marie Higgins (8)
Bamford Primary School

THE WHY POEM

I am just going up the stairs
Why?
Because I'm going to decorate
Why?
Because visitors are coming
Why?
Because it's Christmas
Why?
Because it's December
Why?
Teatime
Why?
High time you stopped saying why.

William Mackey (8)
Bamford Primary School

MY HOLIDAY

The sun beams on me,
When I'm on my holiday,
On my little boat.

When I have a drink,
The birds knock my drink over,
On my holiday.

Thomas Jolley (8)
Bamford Primary School

Don't Call King Cobra Hissy-Head Till You Cross The Desert

Call king cobra hissy-head,
Call king cobra back-bone body,
Call king cobra umbrella-head,
Call king cobra starey-eyes,
Call king cobra hissy-brain,
Call king cobra man-eater maniac,
Call king cobra all those rude words
But you'd better wait
Till you cross the desert.

Andrew Randall (8)
Bamford Primary School

What Am I?

Shaped as a deep cylinder,
Size, 100 metres long,
1000 years old,
Found deep underground,
I sound like drops of water,
My friends are lights,
My enemies are stones,
I wish people would stop walking inside me,
I am a cave.

Stephen Hollis (8)
Bamford Primary School

WHAT AM I?

I am the shape of a stegosaurus,
I am 5 hundred feet high,
I am 7 thousand years old,
I am found in the forest,
I make a lot of noise,
My worst enemies are meat-eaters,
I am a T-Rex.

Sam Shelton (9)
Bamford Primary School

WHAT AM I?

I look like a black sausage
I'm about 60cm long
I have a white belly
I can be found underground
I live in a burrow
I eat lettuce
I'm a badger!

Ashley Eastwood (9)
Bamford Primary School

THE SHARK

I am the shark gliding through the icy waters
I feed on fish, big fish
But my favourite food of all is people
Because I am Jaws and
I am waiting for you!

Robert Machon (8)
Bamford Primary School

WHAT AM I?

Young and miserable,
I show sadness in a child
When they are told off or upset,
I make lots of noise,
I live in the eye,
Laughter is my worst enemy,
What am I?
(A tear).

Anna Read (9)
Bamford Primary School

WHAT AM I?

I am born in the sky,
I am very wet and quite small,
'Splash' I am going really fast,
Over a rock past a sparkly fish,
Past the swamp, up and down,
I am finally there,
What am I?

Thomas Spence (9)
Bamford Primary School

WHAT AM I?

I pound the snow churning it up,
I am round and soft and white,
I have four legs,
I live underground,
I feed on seals and fish,
I swim in a cold sea.

Robert Silcocks (9)
Bamford Primary School

WHAT AM I?

I sail the Milky Way,
I swirl through moon and stars,
I dodge shooting rockets,
I let off glittery smoke,
I love the way I wail,
I go up to the moon,
I go to Mars,
I dodge planets,
Can you guess what I am?
I am a rocket!

Daisy Biney (9)
Bamford Primary School

THE JOURNEY OF A RIVER

Hurling over rocks, falling down the falls,
Bubbling at the bottom,
Breaking into a thousand pieces,
Getting faster and faster,
Slipping, spitting, swirling, spluttering, sliding,
Tackling trees with its mighty arms,
Faster and faster,
Over rocks, down a hill
And there, free into the open sea.

David Perkins (9)
Bamford Primary School

WHAT AM I?

I'm white and fluffy,
I'm quite small but I will be big,
I'm never cold, but you would be,
That's because I live in the Arctic Circle,
I try to catch fish but fall into the icy waters,
I'm three weeks old,
I have fur,
What am I?
A polar bear cub.

Jessica Wing (10)
Bamford Primary School

WHAT AM I?

Black as night,
Cannot be seen,
Hunting prey,
All small and fluffy,
But can grow quite big,
They roam with a pack,
What am I?
I am a baby panther.

Lucy Wing (10)
Bamford Primary School

I'VE GONE SOMEWHERE WEIRD

I've gone somewhere weird,
You can stand on the sea,
For I've gone somewhere weird.

I've gone somewhere weird,
You can't climb a tree because it's slippery,
For I've gone somewhere weird.

I've gone somewhere weird,
You cannot eat anything,
For I've gone somewhere weird.

I've gone somewhere weird,
But now I'm leaving Plastic Land,
For I've gone somewhere weird.

Eoin Loveless (9)
Bamford Primary School

QUESTIONS

What shape are you? Pointy
What size are you? 18 feet
How old are you? I am 100 years old
How big is your mouth? Very big
Do you live in the deep water? Yes I do.

Jake Magee (9)
Bamford Primary School

WHAT AM I?

What shape are you? An oval shape.
What size are you? Any size.
How old are you? 1000 years old.
Where can you be found? On a ship.
What sounds can you make? Oooooo.
Who are your friends and neighbours? No one.
Who is your enemy? The sucker person.
What do you wish for? I wish I was alive.

What am I?
I am a ghost.

Jonathan Todd (9)
Bamford Primary School

THE DOLPHIN

As blue as the morning sky,
Diving deep, deep down to tiny fish,
Doing tricks through hoops,
Their spray is like a shower of rain,
Fins as sharp as a needle.

Alexandra Joan Winder (9)
Bamford Primary School

UNTITLED

I live on fish
I have a pointy fin
I live in deep water
I have built-in radar
Watch out for me.

Luke Somerset (9)
Bamford Primary School

WHAT AM I?

I am big and brown,
I live in the jungle,
I can rustle the leaves on the ground,
My family are monkeys and gorillas,
I wish humans wouldn't chop down trees,
What am I?
A baboon.

Heidi Kearsey (8)
Bamford Primary School

DWIGHT YORKE

Ball pounder,
Ball passer,
Ball tackler,
Ball dribbler,
Goal scorer,
Non fouler,
Fair player,
Wide grinner,
Sweat pourer,
Strong kicker,
Speedy runner.

Jack Wood (10)
Bonsall CE Primary School

MY SMALL GOLDFISH!

M is for mini holes that he swims through,
Y is for yucky mess he makes.

S is for stones in the bottom of the tank,
M is for Max, the name of my goldfish,
A is for algae that grows in his pond,
L is for limbering underneath his bridge,
L is for lonely, he swims on his own.

G is for gills that he uses to breathe,
O is for orange, the colour of his scales,
L is for laughter, the joy that he brings,
D is for diving deep in his tank,
F is for fins which help him to swim,
I is for interest as he swims through his caves,
S is for swimming, he does it all day,
H is for happiness he has all the time.

Holly Strawford (11)
Bonsall CE Primary School

ME AND LADY

I must go and ride a horse
and I will call her Lady.
I will ride her in the fields
and I will keep her forever.
I won't let anyone ride her,
I'll ride her every day,
I'll love her and she'll love me
and I will feed her lots of hay.

Cleo Elizabeth Strawford (9)
Bonsall CE Primary School

GHOSTS

On a silent night in December,
In the ancient creepy mansion,
Something took place that no one remembers,
Abandoned except for one lonely man.

Crackling, three transparent shapes appeared,
Floating, creeping around the old armour,
Not so silently, the man peered,
At three faces burnt and scarred.

At twelve precisely there came a scream,
A glinting silver knife twitched,
The white face all nasty and mean,
A high cruel laugh and the man was gone.

Peter Randall (10)
Bonsall CE Primary School

FORTY WINKS

Stalking up on prey
Jumping, pouncing
Rolling, bouncing
In the endless grass
In a flash
It leaps to catch the mouse
But fails in its longless attempts
It turns and twists in the shade
While having forty winks.

Amy Rickards (11)
Bonsall CE Primary School

ROBOT WARS

It's Friday night. 'Is it time yet, Dad?'
We all sit round, my brother and me.

We've waited all week and rushed our tea,
'Let the wars begin,' shouts Craig.

Robots smashing
Metal mashing
Blades lashing

And Sir Killalot's pincer gnashing
And the whole arena crashing,
Come on let's play - Destroy and Slay.

Who will win and who's going in the bin?

Robots smashing
Wheels trashing
Arena bashing
And pit crashing

But Craig thinks you can keep your Chihuahuas
And your cute Labradors cos we only have
Pitbulls on Robot Wars!

Lawrence Wright (8)
Bonsall CE Primary School

THE ONLY CHANCE

A foot took me down
Suddenly the ball spun wide
I looked up, I'd missed.

Simon Johnson (10)
Bonsall CE Primary School

NORA

She's quiet and lazy
Snoring by day
Golden and fluffy
In her bed she stays
It's gone dark
We hear a noise
Spin, spin, spin
The wheel is her toy
Into her food bowl she dives
Her pouches are filled
Storing nuts and fruit,
Oh! She is alive
She's Nora, my hamster.

Callum Robinson (9)
Bonsall CE Primary School

JELLY BEAN THE GUINEA PIG

Black, white with pink paws,
she scrabbles with her white claws.
Dives into the hay so wide,
this is where she likes to hide.

Chloe Brunton-Dunn (8)
Bonsall CE Primary School

THE MIST

Spookily, quietly falls the mist,
As the hawthorn pricks my wrist.
The mist hangs over the city,
I hear a little girl cry with pity.
I quickly go back to my house,
On the way I see a little mouse.

Rebecca Smith (9)
Bonsall CE Primary School

HOSTAGE

Imprisoned in a cheerless, dismal cell,
Petrifying thoughts dwelling in my mind.
To escape, my head will story-make,
Up, up into the clouds -
Imagination
Is my
Golden key.
My childhood appears
Innocently from my mind,
So that I escape reality.
I am free now, no boundaries for me,
Here on my voyage of imagination.

Caroline Brown (9)
Brassington Primary School

THE DARE

The day they dared me to do this thing,
I went dizzy and my ears began to ring.
What should I do? Excuses pounded through my head,
I just wanted to curl up in my cosy bed.

It really was an awful dare,
Nobody liked me so they didn't care.
Nobody thought I was trendy and cool,
Just because I was new at school.

They jeered and laughed and called me chicken,
But to this dare I wasn't stickin'.
I fought with words and said, 'No way'
They couldn't make me anyway.

I didn't reply,
I didn't cry,
It was no joke,
They actually dared me to try and smoke.

Siân Hughes (10)
Chinley Primary School

SADNESS

Sadness is a bluey-grey
It smells like damp leaves
It sounds like wailing wind
It tastes like sour milk
It feels wet and soggy
It lives under the sea.

Siobhan Connolly (9)
Chinley Primary School

BALLAD OF BETH GÊLERT

The prince returned to his faithful hound,
And walked right through the door,
To his surprise he looked around,
And couldn't believe the gore.

He cried for his child,
'Where is my baby?'
He looked like a bull, wild,
Under the blanket maybe?

In his eyes water filled,
He murdered his friendly dog,
His loyal dog, the wolf killed,
Llewellyn felt lost like a wounded hog.

Andrew Paul Loynes (10)
Chinley Primary School

ANIMALS, ANIMALS

Animals, animals big and small
Some are short and some are tall
Some are slick and some are sly
Some are tough and some cry

Animals are fluffy but some are rough
Some are flat and some go puff
Some are silly and some are smooth
Some are dry and some are wet
And some are pets.

Hayley Wheelton (9)
Chinley Primary School

ANIMALS

Horses, pigs and cats
sleep in the night,
unlike foxes, owls and bats
who sleep in the light.

Fish, whales and frogs
go down to the deep,
but hamsters, cows and dogs
always like to sleep.

Worms, rats and mice
always like the damp,
but rabbits, gerbils and lice
like it near the lamp.

Georgie Beeley (9)
Chinley Primary School

THE THING

The thing on my arms is as heavy as a rock,
The thing on my arms is as fat as a pig,
The thing on my arms has a smelly sock,
The thing on my arms has a crazy wig.

The thing on my arms has a tall mum and dad,
The thing on my arms has a wet nappy,
The thing on my arms has a brother who's bad,
The thing on my arms is happy,
The thing on my arms is a baby.

Matthew Wheeldon (10)
Chinley Primary School

MY GRANDAD

He goes to the pub every night,
He's very funny and is half-bald as a sheep and tells jokes,
Sometimes we go for walks and we collect conkers,
He says, 'Go and tell your gran that you are lost'
And I go, 'OK.'
At night when we are watching TV he goes to sleep and he snores,
And in his sleep he blows bubbles.

But best of all he takes me to the
Sweet shop.

Ryan Trickett (9)
Chinley Primary School

WAR POEM

War is dark green
tastes like rotten eggs
smells like strong sprouts
war is very grumbly and grumpy
feels very unhappy
war lives in a cave.

Lives in the scariest forest yet
where no man even dreams to go
but it is very wet
scariest creature yet.

Nathan Parry (9)
Chinley Primary School

THE MIGHTY MACHINE

The train on the track
Clickety clack
On the track
Clickety clack.

Screeching to a halt
Oh no, there's a fault
Screeching to a halt
There is a fault.

Clicking of handbags
Tearing of rags
Clicking handbags
Tearing rags.

People chattering
Windows shattering
People chattering
Windows shattering.

The mighty machine goes
As smooth as a boat rows
The mighty machine goes
As smooth as a boat rows.

Jacob Burton (10)
Chinley Primary School

THE 1970s

French skipping was cool,
ABBA was in,
No one liked high school,
Kids made a din.

Ankles would sweat,
Bill and Ben were sweet,
Sweets were ate,
Knee-high boots to cover your feet.

Grace Gager (10)
Chinley Primary School

GRANDPA

My grandpa is always watching TV,
He's as dozy as a worm,
Never listening and sleeps like an
Animal in hibernation.

Funny, always playing cards,
As good at maths as a maths teacher,
Eating vegetables like a horse.

He talks all the time,
Says it's bedtime at 8 o'clock,
Cleans the garden like a gardener,
He plays football like a champion.

My grandpa wears trainers all the time,
He's very funny
And has the memory of an elephant,
Tidies up like Noo-Noo
And best of all he takes me to
The beach and castles.

He lives in Wales about two hours away,
We often go down to the bay,
The Punch and Judy is often on.

William Kerr (8)
Chinley Primary School

SCHOOL

Pens, pencils, books,
Pens, pencils, books,
The teacher's gone mad,
But her husband passed away
And now she's really sad,
Well, that's what they say,
Pens, pencils, books.

Pens, pencils, books,
Pens, pencils, books,
I hate you
You hit me on the head,
Now I want to sue,
I think that's what I said,
Pens, pencils, books.

Pens, pencils, books,
Pens, pencils, books,
The school set on fire,
But the flames came yesterday,
The fire engine got a flat tyre
And can only come today,
Now there's no pens, pencils or books.

Leonie Wharmby (10)
Chinley Primary School

WHEN LLEWELLYN KILLED HIS DOG

The day Llewellyn killed his dog,
He stabbed him in the side,
So he thought of buying another dog,
Then he said he lied.

Llewellyn could hear the cry
And he could feel the pain,
Then he gave a sigh
And thought he was insane.

Kyle Gill (10)
Chinley Primary School

MY UNCLE ROWLAND

My uncle Rowland is as tall as a tree,
He is very kind to me.
He is as bald as a peeled potato,
He tells me stories and lets me stay for tea.

When he goes on walks he goes on long ones,
Like a hiker who goes 100 miles.

He gives me chocolate, he fixes my bike,
I know him and he is very nice.

He lets me stay over at his house,
A bit like a hotel but with no waiter.

He tells good jokes,
Just like a clown.

He likes to eat potatoes,
He likes to eat jam,
He likes to eat gammon
And he likes to eat ham.

But best of all he gives me chocolate ice cream.

Tom Wild (8)
Chinley Primary School

THE MINOTAUR AND THESEUS

A fierce monster covered in hair,
As brown as a bull, scary as a bear,
Bones in his mouth, crunching every second,
Lurking in his maze, howling in every passage.

Theseus is carrying his mighty sword,
Swinging from side to side.

They met together in the dark, dark maze,
Blood splurting everywhere, howling
Like a wolf, screaming
In the sky.

His maze is leaking, dripping from the roof,
Screaming, thumping in the
Maze, dark like paint.

As hungry as a vulture,
Looking for its dinner.

Theseus is as smart as a growling lion.

Daniel Thomas Wheeldon (8)
Chinley Primary School

ROMANCE

Romance is sparkly,
It smells like wine,
It tastes like strawberries,
Romance sounds like love,
It feels like a warm velvet cushion,
Romance lives in the hearts of kind people.

Hannah Radcliffe (10)
Chinley Primary School

MEDUSA AND PERSEUS

Medusa's eyes as red as a blazing fire
Trying to turn people to stone.
Her hair is as slimy, slippy, surprising
As a gargoyle falling through the cave wall.
Perseus is as handsome as a prince in a
Fairy tale with shining golden armour.
He is as brutal as a great white shark
Slashing his sword around her neck.
Medusa is as sly as a fox
Sneaking out of a rubbish dump,
With bones in her mouth.
She is as wicked as a cackling hyena,
Lingering for something to kill!
He is as hulking as a muscular rhino,
Charging down a herd.
As brave as a prowling lion,
Creeping quietly through the cave.

Rachel Winterbottom (8)
Chinley Primary School

THE GROUND

Deep in the ground little and low,
Who can tell us what they know?
Slimy snails slither around
And a mole in a little mound,
Deep in the ground little and low,
Who can tell us what they know?

James Ellis (9)
Chinley Primary School

MY GRANDAD

My grandad is as bald as an elephant
As slim as a piece of paper

My grandad acts like a chimpanzee in a bad mood
He tells brilliant jokes

My grandad wears jeans that have been in his family for decades
His T-shirts were once white but now they're green

My grandad tells stories about his wife that you can tell aren't true
And he says he has a pet piranha in the pond

My grandad eats sheep's heart sandwiches
And drinks twenty bottles of lager a day

My grandad loves to go horse riding and racing

But best of all he loves me.

Paul Smith (9)
Chinley Primary School

DEATH

Death is sad, death is good,
Death is not healthy as can be,
Death is bad but can be good,
If death was good it would be nice,
Death is like a red hot volcano,
That is death.

David O'Gorman (10)
Chinley Primary School

THE SWEETIE POEM

Fruit Pastilles, Bursting Bugs and strawberry lollipops
Smarties, jelly babies and massive peardrops
Beefburgers, hot dogs and happy smiley faces
Fried eggs, Coca-Cola bottles and big strawberry laces
Chocolate, Time Outs, Twixs and Twirls
Maltesers, Breakaways and gorgeous Galaxy Swirls
Chocolate Buttons and magic Milky Way stars
Bubblegum, Minstrels and a chocolatey Mars
Liquorice allsorts and gooey Milky Ways
If you go in the shop the shopkeeper says
'Everybody please come into my shop' but he didn't say
Anything else because he turned into a chocolate drop.

Melissa Grindey (10)
Chinley Primary School

WILD ANIMALS

Iguanas are colourful,
splatted with paint.

Tigers are stripy
like iguanas ain't.

Leopards are spotty
and fast like a cheetah!
And when they run they get hot like a heater.

Gorillas are hairy unlike a fairy.

All wild animals are just great,
and sometimes like my best mate!

Alice Duncan (10)
Chinley Primary School

My Grandma

My grandma is nice and kind,
She eats yoghurt, meat and sweetcorn.

Jumper, trousers and T-shirt,
Sleep, eat and snore.

Funny, nice and beautiful,
Fight for the bed with Tosh the cat.

Are you enjoying your mashed potato?

Gam likes to play football,
And is nice as a teddy bear.

When my mummy will not let me buy anything,
Gam always buys me it.

Laura Scowcroft (8)
Chinley Primary School

My Dog, Scruffy

As brown as wet mud
As cuddly as a big, fluffy bear
As cute as a rabbit
As floppy as a piece of rubber
As furry as a chinchilla
As interesting as a video game
As funny as a comedian.

But at least
He's mine!

Katie Lee (9)
Chinley Primary School

MY GRANDAD

My grandad has big glasses and a bald head
His voice is as loud as a *foghorn*
He likes to give advice

He says, 'Eat your tomatoes
They will make you very strong'

My grandad plays badminton
He says he's really good at it

My grandad makes delicious scones
But best of all he lets me feed the fish.

James Sweetman (8)
Chinley Primary School

FAT CAT

He's big, he's fat,
he's huge, he's enormous,
because he's fat cat.
He's so big he can't
fit through the door.
He's porky, he's smart,
but fat. He eats cakes,
buns, sweets, chocolate,
crisps, chips and sausages,
but no fruit because he's
fat cat!

Bradley Weston (9)
Chinley Primary School

MY GRANDMA

My grandma's hair is as tangled as a bush
She is as nice as my mum
She cooks dinners fit for a king

My grandma leans over to walk like a meerkat
She is as clean as a bird
She eats vegetables like a chimpanzee

My grandma is as wrinkled as a paper bag
She behaves as good as gold
She wears expensive clothes like stars

My grandma says I'm as good as gold too
She likes resting after a hard day's work, like my dad
But best of all, she gives us sweets, like my grandad.

William Langman (9)
Chinley Primary School

DIPLODOCUS POEM

Hocus pocus, plodding through the swamp, I'm a diplodocus,
chomp, chomp, chomp, grass for breakfast, I can eat a tree,
grass for lunch and dinner and grass for tea.
Hocus pocus, I'm a diplodocus going through the forest,
jump, jump, I saw a new diplodocus.
Hocus pocus, I'm a diplodocus going through the wood
and I got stuck in some mud.

Nathan Porter (10)
Chinley Primary School

THE MIDNIGHT HORSE

Cautiously after the moon slips about,
the midnight horse comes galloping out,
and radiant beams of light shall meet:
the weary, thudding of thy feet.

After seconds of muscles, rippling in waves,
he canters into the midnight caves:
and there he stands all alone,
but is he? Does he hear a moan?

Many nights the field is clear,
is it a horse or is it a deer?
So much for a midnight, moonlit night:
the horse and its rider begin to fight . . .

Further and further into the battle,
hooves thudding like runaway cattle . . .
cautiously after the moon slips about
the midnight horse comes galloping out.

Islay Mackinlay (11)
Chinley Primary School

SUN POEM

The sun, brighter than a flower, it makes you look beautiful,
every morning it wakes you up, it is like a buttercup.
Yellowy than ever, the sun comes out orange every morning,
it makes you get up and go downstairs and
have breakfast and go to school looking like a star.

John James Simpson (10)
Chinley Primary School

MY GRANDMA

My grandma is as small as a mouse,
She behaves like a cat,
She likes to feed animals,
My grandma wears a skirt.

She likes to eat pies,
She says that I am nice,
She likes to go shopping
And going to garden centres.

My grandma is funny
And as thin as a carrot,
She is as warm as an oven,
But I like her best for being there for me!

Kirsty Osbaldiston (8)
Chinley Primary School

FAT CAT

He's big, he's fat, he's porky because he's fat cat.
He's rich, oh no it's fat cat.
He's really cool because he's fat cat.
He's too big to fit through the cat flap.
He's smart because he's fat cat.
He eats chocolate and lovely raspberry ripple cakes.
He jumps in the bath, it's not water, it's chocolate.
He even eats it.
His house is made out of sweets and chocolate because he's fat cat.

Ryan Appleby (9)
Chinley Primary School

WHEN I WAS IN CLASS

When I was in class,
I was asked to write a poem,
If I pass
I can have 10 house points.

But I can't do the poem Miss,
Why?
Cause I've got to look after my sis,
But she just said don't be silly.

So I got on with the rhyme,
But this is all I've done so far.
Once I ate a piece of lime,
I know it is very silly.

But I never finished it,
So I was very sad,
And was in the pit
Of shame.

William Simpson (10)
Chinley Primary School

TROUBLESOME PETS!

Paw prints, paw prints
Muddy, messy dints
Miaow, woof, squeak
What a lot of leaks.

Toys flying in the air
Chewing, scratching everywhere
Miaow, woof, squeak
What a lot of leaks.

Lizzie Ripley (10)
Chinley Primary School

THE MONSTER

The hissing hair
Scared me when I went into the lair of Medusa

Past the ghouls and suddenly
There stood the monster
I had to be aware
Because she could turn people
To stone

I used my mirror and what a surprise
She turned to stone .

And that was the *end*
Of Medusa.

Jennifer Sweetman (8)
Chinley Primary School

MY GRANDMA

My grandma is a kind, understanding girl
With a face like a pretty angel,
She has blue forget-me-not eyes and nice farming clothes.
Her hair is as grey as a rain cloud.
Her voice does not sound very loud.
She sits on her chair every day and reads.
She sometimes cooks my dinner and it tastes wonderful,
So wonderful I normally eat it all.
She brews me cups of tea and I drink them all.
She gives me presents and little toys.
She is a lovely grandma.

Hannah Wood (8)
Chinley Primary School

MY GRANDPA

My grandpa wears a suit and tie like a business man,
He likes eating chocolate in bed,
Dark blue eyes like a stormy sea.

Counting money like a teacher,
He makes me giggle like a hyena,
He is a giggle a lot grandpa,
Looking after my gran.

Time ticks away when he is at the bus stop,
Counting sheep in his dream of long ago when he was young.

He loves to take a nap on the chair like a cat near the fire.

Hannah Wallace (9)
Chinley Primary School

MY GRANDPA

My grandpa's face looks crinkled like a bin bag.
He sits in his chair all day sometimes.
He likes to say, 'Come on, let's go.'
He wears a brown coat and grey trousers.
He eats soup and spaghetti.
He smokes like a train.
He can run faster than a rocket.
He sleeps like a baby.
He can kick a ball for a mile.
He walks like a bear.

He is a nice person.

Liam Groarke (9)
Chinley Primary School

MEDUSA AND PERSEUS

Medusa is as hairy as a bear,
She is a tiger growling at an opponent.

She is a horrible, slimy monster turning
People into stone as they look at her.
She is as smelly as rubbish being put into a dustbin.
Her hair is as tough as rope.
She is a really brave gorgon when she's battling.
She is as loud as a big base drum.

Perseus is as evil as a Minotaur.
He is a brave, bulky beast battling Medusa with his sword.
He's a muscular monster killer lurking in the dark night
With his big mighty weapons.

Beth Goddard (9)
Chinley Primary School

GRANDMA POEM

My grandma sits like an old gorilla talking all day,
She is as wrinkled as an old elephant.

My grandma is as slow as a water snail,
She is as small as a teenage rat,
She is as intelligent as a teacher,
She is as tired as a giraffe that's been eating all day,
But best of all she is as nice as a flower!

Joe Hall (9)
Chinley Primary School

MEDUSA AND PERSEUS

Her eyes as black as burning coal,
Slyly spying in her lair, stiffening
People with her eyes.
Perseus is as muscular as a rhino
Charging on the plain.
Slimy, slippy, slinky snakes spitting in her hair.

She is as dangerous as a lioness on the prowl,
Perseus is a handsome, husky hare
Bounding around the labyrinth.
She's a towering white-toothed polar bear.

Hannah Collins (9)
Chinley Primary School

MY GRANDMA

My grandma is as kind as a charity girl who stays day and night
Collecting money for poorly children,
She is as small as a hare,
She is as friendly as my friendly guinea pig.

She wears more cardigans than a girl who tries on
Different cardigans every day,
She gives me more 50ps than my mum does on my birthday,
She likes to go to the garden centre more than any other grandma.

Annabel Jones (9)
Chinley Primary School

MY GRANDPA

My grandpa tells stories like a well-known poet.
He is as bald as an egg.
He is as funny as a circus clown.
He eats egg on toast.
He could be an actor like James Bond.
He thinks his car is a dream.
He is like Inspector Gadget.
He always whistles like a bird.
He is always there for me like soil in the ground
When you are planting a flower,
And best of all, he always lets me help him.

Louissa Wragg (9)
Chinley Primary School

GRANDPA JOHN

My grandpa John is as plump as Father Christmas,
He peers over his spectacles and snoozes in his chair,
Only coming out for meals.

My grandpa John eats meat as ravenously as a lion,
He covers potatoes with his stomach like the ground.

My grandpa John plods about like a rhino and
Best of all he is nice and cuddly like a bear.

Rhiannon Hughes (8)
Chinley Primary School

FREEDOM

When I'm sad and lonely
I simply have no choice,
But to go outside riding
Upon my dainty horse.

As I gallop over fields,
I feel the wind in my hair,
It pushes out awful feelings
And lets me relax instead.

As I canter over streams,
The water hits my heels,
I feel so lucky inside
To be able to let go of my fears.

As my ride is ending,
The sunset's overhead,
I feel so free and lively,
As I retreat to my lonely bed.

Holly Smith (11)
Chinley Primary School

MY GRANDPA ROY

My grandpa is as fun as a fair,
Every morning he pretends to shave me with his shaver,
He had a gold tooth,
My grandpa is as warm as a tumble-dryer,
My grandpa is really nice,
But best of all I love him.

Paige Amy Holland (8)
Chinley Primary School

DAYS OF DISMAY, PIECES OF PLEASURE

Even though you must not dismay,
It is just another day,
People walk across the way,
Just another day in May.

I just sleep in my bed, on my head a cap,
As I settle for a long winter's nap,
I sleep all the day,
For awake I dismay.

A day that is cold,
A ninja stands bold,
Two metal workers begin to mould
A dismal day in May.

I watch soundly as a bird,
Watching a computer nerd,
As he programs
A cold day in May.

Dogs run home,
To get their tasty juicy bone,
I watch silently as a turtle,
I started to forget my dismay.

I turned over in my bed
And stabbed myself with pencil lead,
As quickly as a tiger,
I wake up on a sunny day in June.

June, June, like a magic boon,
As pleasurable as a lagoon
And as watchable as a cartoon.

Thank God! It is once again June.

Joe Forster (10)
Chinley Primary School

RUN TIGER, RUN

As he places the tiger onto his truck
He turns his back and hears a roar
The tiger is still alive
It leaps with a slight limp
Onto the poacher who falls.

Off the tiger runs
Stripes and all
Back to his home
Then he sleeps
He awakes to hunt once again
His life is back to normal once again.

Emily Wild (11)
Chinley Primary School

MY GRANDAD ROY

My grandad Roy is nice,
He is grumpy when I am naughty,
He is careful with his shaver
As smart as a fox
And he buys me treats,
But the best thing of all is
I love him and he is the best grandad in the world.

Leigh Ann Holland (8)
Chinley Primary School

THE JOB INTERVIEW

I wrote it down
Just saying no
But then it happened
Shall I go?

Nothing to write
Nothing to say
I'm going crazy
But it's today

My head is floating far
My hands are dropping dead
Help me, please help me
I'll have to see doctor Fred

Say I get it wrong
What will I do?
I might ask someone
Maybe you.

I'll say one thing
I'm not scared of heights
But at this moment
I'm seeing bright lights.

Tom Lomas (10)
Chinley Primary School

DEATH

Death is slimy, bad and dark, is how he's seen
He smells of old socks and eggs
If you taste him you would go green
Death sounds like a choked person with shaky legs

He feels like lava really hot
He sneaks around sly and cross
He's just found a bed in an orange pot
Death is going to kill Ross.

Zoe Berk (9)
Chinley Primary School

THE BARMY TEACHER

Clock's ticking, what's flicking?
Miss, Miss, Jack's sticking
Bell's gone, carry on.

That table's unstable
What's that, a stable?
No Miss, it's Jack's sis.

Bell's rung, someone's wrong
Dinner time, that's right
What a kite.

Stephanie Griffiths (10)
Chinley Primary School

THE GIRL WHO COULD FLY

There was a young girl who could fly
Whose favourite good was meat pie
She ate and she ate
And then met her fate
When the pie it fell *splat!* from the sky.

Emma Lowe (11)
Chinley Primary School

DINNER TIME

Fat chips,
Cold custard,
Roast ham,
No mustard.

Children talking,
Children walking,
Children chewing,
Children booing.

Lips smacking,
Fingers cracking,
Happy faces
In their places.

Aeroplane trays,
Children play,
Roast potatoes,
Fat red tomatoes.

Line up,
Get your cup,
Grab a plate,
Don't be late.

Chairs clanging,
Knives and forks banging,
All in a rush,
Not much hush.

Lots of noise,
From girls and boys,
Munching, munching,
Crunching, crunching.

Now it's over, time to go,
Out we play, rain, wind or snow.

Luke Reynolds (10)
Chinley Primary School

THESEUS AND THE MINOTAUR

Glinting, sharp horns glowing in the dark.
As repulsive as a witch making her magic potion.
Licking its hungry lips, waiting for its dinner.
As bold as a pirate charging into battle.
A handsome, brave young man brandishing his sword.
He is a leopard searching its prey.

Tobin Carey-Williams (8)
Chinley Primary School

MINOTAUR AND THESEUS

In the cave it's creepy, weepy and it makes you sleepy.
It's a bull, it stabs its horns and oscillates his horns.
He waits and wiggles for a tear.
It eats your liver like a bear.
Poking his sword into monsters,
He swings his sword like a lion's tail,
He's a snake, he did it quick.

Tom Booth (9)
Chinley Primary School

SUPERMARKET NIGHTMARE

When I take Timmy shopping,
It is always a nightmare.
Unfortunately, I have to take him twice a week,
He sits there looking sweet and cute
And being good as gold,
Until we go past the baked beans that is;
He glances, then glances again,
His eyes bulge, he reaches out,
Only I sweep the trolley away just in time.
Beans, beans, beans, beans!
He cries like some deprived child,
'Beans' he cries again,
Everybody stares and some tut-tut,
But they don't know the real Timmy,
They think he's just some cute baby.
'Come on' I say, now to the fruit and veg,
I put a lettuce in, he throws it out;
It lands among the apples,
I try putting a cucumber in the trolley,
Only he just kicks it out, as he's in a mood now.
'OK, OK, we'll get some beans' I say.
His face lights up, a gleam appears,
He waves his arms around as if in applause,
When I place the beans in the trolley,
He wails 'More, more' and then he starts to whimper,
So it all starts all over again . . .
If anybody would like to volunteer to look after Timmy
Whilst I go to the supermarket,
Then it would be most welcome!

Amy Pickles (10)
Chinley Primary School

DUGGIE GROSSIBLE

There once was a burglar whose name was Duggie Grossible.
He sneaked into people's homes whenever it was possible.

One day he went to a house and opened the fine old door,
When all at once there was a shot - and he fell upon the floor.

Then along came the police, who arrested the unknown killer,
And he turned out to be a disgustingly ugly old miller.

He was sentenced to life in jail, kept on water and rotten bread,
But they didn't seem to notice him, and never was he fed.

So one day he died and was put into a grave,
But one of the policemen said, 'He'd 'ave made a brilliant slave!'

So that was the end of them two, and never did they come back,
For they were very dead and under the ground in a sack.

But one day their spirit will return and haunt the boys in blue,
And if you're very unlucky, they might come and haunt you too!

So, always be on the lookout and never close your eyes,
Because it will be your final move - apart from your death cries.

The people you should look out for are the burglar Duggie Grossible,
Who sneaked into people's homes whenever it was possible.

You should also look out for the disgustingly ugly old miller,
Who still to this day is known as 'The Mysterious Unknown Killer'.

So, whenever you are anywhere keep your eyes peeled open wide,
For old Duggie Grossible and the killer who is now on his side.

Omid Kashan (10)
Chinley Primary School

THE MINOTAUR

The Minotaur is a blood-thirsty monster,
Crunching fresh bones.
Head of a bull,
Body of 1000 Greek wrestlers put together.
Horns sharp as 10 knives.
Theseus ready to chop and slice the
Minotaur up into little pieces.
Ready to crush and
Mush the Minotaur's bones.
Theseus has defeated the mighty monster
And carries his bloody
Sword up the tunnel.

Bill Richmond (8)
Chinley Primary School

PERRY THE PEREGRINE

There was a peregrine called Perry,
Who wore an oversized beret,
He said he could fly,
But it was a big lie,
And he crash-landed down in Delhi.

Oliver Theaker (10)
Chinley Primary School

THESEUS AND THE MINOTAUR

Fit flesh fighting giant beast
Huge handsome hunting meat
Shining shivering monster killing hero
A bulky big brave man
Walking near Minotaur
Greedy grizzly hairy monster
Howling hungry in the labyrinth
Waiting for its dinner.

Elizabeth Dakin (9)
Chinley Primary School

MEDUSA AND PERSEUS

Slithering, sliding, slippery,
Skulking in her lair,
She is as smooth as a serpent,
Gliding through an underground cave.
Medusa is a troll that has never had a bath.

Perseus is a brave bull fighting for its life,
Handsome as a king, just been crowned.
A hulking, saving, serving hero.

Hannah Tattersfield (9)
Chinley Primary School

THERE WAS A MAN FROM CHINA

There was a man from China
He lived on a dock
He travelled the world as a climber
He slipped on a rock
And broke his clock
It caused him so much pain
He couldn't work a digital clock
And now he's gone insane.

David Harding (9)
Chinley Primary School

THE MINOTAUR

Strong as a charging bull,
Tough as a shark,
Muscular as a boxer,
Fighting in the ring.

Wild as a tiger,
Raving like a rhino,
Ferocious as a lion,
Chasing a frightened zebra.

Corrina Wilson (9)
Chinley Primary School

DOUGHNUTS

Ten little doughnuts sitting in a line
Along came a gorilla
And then there were nine!

Nine little doughnuts sitting on a plate
One rolled off a cliff
And then there were eight!

Eight little doughnuts floating in Heaven
Along came me and then there were seven!

Seven little doughnuts eating a Twix
Along came a builder and then there were six!

Six little doughnuts barely alive
Along came Thomas and then there were five!

Five little doughnuts having a war
One got shot and then there were four!

Four little doughnuts looking at me
Along came Amy and then there were three!

Three little doughnuts sitting on the loo
One fell down and then there were two!

Two little doughnuts that weigh a ton
Mrs Gent ate one and then there was one!

Joseph Shaw (8)
Codnor CE Junior School

THE LAST ONE

At first there was a tiny neighing
From a tiny mouth,
In the wind his mane was swaying,
The wind was blowing south.

On his head starting to grow,
Was a golden horn,
On his head it started to glow,
Like it did the day he was born.

Drinking from the Rainbow River,
Looks up, then takes another,
The wind gets cold, he starts to shiver,
Snuggles up close to his mother.

Days go by he's starting to grow,
His mane all soft and silky,
His horn is big it's starting to glow,
His fur all white and milky.

His mother is ill; she needs a friend,
All droopy and delicate her head,
It's not OK, this day's her end,
It's too late; she's already dead.

Two years have passed and all is well,
His horn, nearly fully grown,
All this time he will not tell,
He will not say, he will not moan.

Three years have passed; he's found a mate,
He's got a good life now,
His horn is tall, he couldn't wait
For it to grow, but how?

One year has passed, back in the wood,
By huntsmen his mate was killed;
The Rainbow River was in a flood,
His heart was sorrowfully filled.

Five years later he's growing old,
He's trying to make it home,
The winter wind is very cold,
Very lonely when you're alone.

And there in his sleep he peacefully dies:
So softly, so silently, so nice,
And the look of love is in his eyes,
If only he lived twice.

Rebecca Stevenson (11)
Codnor CE Junior School

COLOURS

The colour red is like the sunset,
The colour green is like unripened tomatoes,
The colour blue is like navy jeans,
The colour yellow is like the sun,
The colour pink is like white people's skin,
The colour purple is like a plum,
The colour white is like paper,
The colour black is like ink,
The colour orange is like the fruit, orange,
The colour grey is like a computer.

Adam Forster (8)
Codnor CE Junior School

THE WIND

The wind is a wild creature
waiting to pounce on innocent victims.
Holding back till the darkness comes.
He smashes and crashes, pulling up the roots of huge trees.
The mighty oak tree falls to his knees
at the strength of the almighty creature.
The deadly beast devouring the land.
Slamming bins at walls, thumping, pounding.
No one can stop it.
Nothing can stand in his way.
Ripping up the Earth,
Destroying people's possessions.
Uncontrollable is the wild, crazy, careless, abnormal
Creature of the skies.

But . . . *stop*
All is silent
until the demon of the dark comes again.
The wind is a wild creature
waiting to pounce on innocent victims.

Sarah Woolley (10)
Codnor CE Junior School

I REMEMBER, I REMEMBER

I remember, I remember
Going to that dreaded place,
The screams, the shouts and the crying,
Working till I'm blue in the face.

I remember, I remember
Going through all the school years,
I found it getting better,
Less and less of the tears.

I remember, I remember
Enjoying it more and more,
Laughing, playing and running,
Even my work wasn't a chore.

I remember, I remember
That my teachers were the best,
My friends were simply brilliant,
My head teacher beat the rest.

Jack Duncan-Handley (11)
Codnor CE Junior School

THE WIND

The wind is a tribe of animals
A dog howling wildly in the crack of every wall,
A racoon stealing menacingly from bins,
A mischievous monkey knocking away happiness,
A giant panda pulling away flowers to eat,
A lion roaring, eating up discarded bricks,
An ape climbing houses and pulling away slates,
A man-eating tiger terrorising women and children,
A long-ago dinosaur eats at buildings,
A strangled cat yelling for hours on end,
A spider scaring and stealing all to find
But a gentle touch from a dolphin or whale,
Will slowly calm just a like a snail,
And the cruel wild tribe will leave,
Leaving all their bad work behind
For humans to repair this nightmare.

Rebecca Rawlinson (10)
Codnor CE Junior School

MY LITTLE BROTHER

Note to readers, he's not a good speller, he's only 2!

Me and my sissy were in garden
And I went to get a ball,
But sissy begin to moan
And make me's fall!

But me's get up and go anyway
Sissy angry then
Then me don't like it
So me go and hid in me's den.

One hour later
Me's came out of den now,
Sissy still steamed up
What was that word again?
Oh yeah, she was like a pup
Another hour later
Me's look out again
Sissy was alright now
But she wanted her own way
And she went *bow wow!*
That frighted me but
Sissy said sorry
And it soon ended
Me's little poem!

Cordelia Jackson (8)
Codnor CE Junior School

THE ASCENT

(Note: Start at bottom and work way up)

And shouted to the world, 'I've done it!'
Then I came upon the summit
Towards the top so off I went
Then got up and I was sent
Almost there then had to stop
Though more mist and to the top
Below freezing point, my senses gone
Then next day I venture on
In my fingers frostbite, cramp
Through the mist and to the camp
Going up and getting colder
Over hills and a huge great boulder
Past dead men with swords and shields
Over black boulders and dew-soaked fields
But the air was cool and courage was found
The day arrived:- The sun beat down

Emma Larkin (10)
Codnor CE Junior School

A RATTLE

Rattle, that silly old battle,
What a rattle, I wish I could end that battle,
Or the rattle
Or could it be some cattle,
Go and get that rattle,
That cattle must be that silly,
Old battle or could it just be a rattle,
Or a battle,
Or some cattle or maybe a
Very big battle.

Thomas Redfern (10)
Darley Dale Primary School

THE RIDE

The child galloped on her horse on a lovely summer's day,
Sheep grazing in a field,
Birds singing their morning song,
Trees flowing gently in the light wind,
The child did not notice the dark clouds above her
Or the trickles of rain in the sky,
She just galloped, galloped, galloped on.
The horse stopped in its tracks as it sensed the danger . . .
But the child urged it on,
'Trot on' she demanded, but without warning the clouds showered
Down rain, the child looked around but nothing looked the same . . .
The child realised how foolish she had been,
Her face was wet with tears and rain,
She walked on nervously and unsure,
The horse winnied as if it sensed her fright.
The rain splattered in her face and her eyes were stinging,
The water hit her and lashed at her like a thousand swords,
She suddenly saw some welcoming lights,
The lights of her home town,
She nearly yelled out in delight,
She promised herself in a whisper, she'd never leave home again.

Ellie Fearn (10)
Darley Dale Primary School

RIVER VOYAGE

The boat invited its last few guests
as it smoothly explored down the stream;
Fish raced the boat in order to win,
it created a marvellous gleam!

People gossiped all the time,
just like a pair of birds would do;
The tulips were dull and looked bored
as if they wanted to come too!

The golden smell of rich food
asked all people to come and eat:
Jam on toast, bacon rolls, ham sandwiches, freshly-baked cookies,
all make the ride a bigger treat!

Now the trip's coming to an end,
people have lovely smiling gleams;
And, as if by magic, slowly and suddenly,
the tired boat makes its way back along the golden stream.

Kelly Thorneycroft (10)
Darley Dale Primary School

A VICIOUS VOYAGE

Up, down, up, down through the wild waves we go,
Up, down, up, down where the wind tosses us to and fro,
The waves are dancing,
The pirates are prancing,
Up, down, up, down.
All off on to dry land,
Umpha, umpha like a brass band;
The seagulls start swooping
And then looping,
Up, down, up, down.
Through the scorching sand,
Of this far-off enchanted land.
What's this I see?
Pass me the key,
Up, down, up, down.
We've found it!
The palm trees are dancing,
I'm prancing,
Up, down, up, down.

Natalie Carline (11)
Darley Dale Primary School

THE TRAVELLER

The moonlight shining silver,
The stars twinkling bright,
Shining upon the traveller
As he walks into the night.
Past the gleaming pond
The traveller carried on,
Until he heard the clock
Chiming half past one.
He came to a deserted cottage
With a tumbled-down old shed,
The thatch was thin and rotten.
As he knocked upon the door
A brown owl's feathers fluttered
And floated down to the floor.
The dog lay asleep in the kennel,
With his paws touching the floor,
The traveller mounted his horse,
As away into the darkness he rode!

Emma Dakin (11)
Darley Dale Primary School

THE MARY ROSE

She left the port with a mighty rumble,
A crew aboard with rats that grumble,
Howling away on that winter's night,
Hoping to see an explorer's sight.

Smelling bodies and filthy hair,
No change of clothes or underwear.
The moon sailed by within the sky,
Now and then letting out a deep sigh.

The food went rotten, which fed the rats,
They became pests and also brats.
They lost their clean water and barrels of beer,
They did not know this but an island was near.

The golden sun highlighted the land,
With palm trees, coconuts and glittery sand.
The animals' sounds brought them no fear,
But the thought of a new island, let out a big cheer!

James Shooter (10)
Darley Dale Primary School

SPACE!

All excitement for the lift-off, there are fireworks everywhere,
But the ten men that are going are panicking everywhere.
They jump into their seats, all shaking like a leaf,
When the call goes out, 3, 2, 1 lift-off,
All fear gone and excitement is in the air.
The journey takes three days or more,
Until they find a moon.
All ten leaped out like little kiddies,
Boing! Boing! All up in the air, flying like ten birds.
They could see for miles and miles
With wonderful colours all around,
Pink, green, blue, colours never even seen before.
Now it is time to go, all ten take souvenirs like powder from rock,
They take off back to Earth and take their rocks out,
All of them are glowing like a star twinkling in the light.

Emma Allen (10)
Darley Dale Primary School

THE FLYING SHIP

Up, up, higher, higher,
Over the hills
And under the moon.
It's the journey of a lifetime,
In a ship that can fly.
Leave the deep blue sea behind
And be with the colourful planets.
The dusty, dirty planets
Where I can jump as high as I want.
I jump back into the ship
And fly over to Jupiter,
Then to Saturn, then to Mars,
But when at night it starts to get cold,
I'll fly back down to Earth,
In my warm cosy bed.
But when the sun shines bright outside,
I'll fly back up to Saturn.

Rachel MacDonald (11)
Darley Dale Primary School

SPACE SHOW

Twirling stars in deep space,
High above the human race.
The planets are blue and green,
It feels like it's only a dream.

Through the blackness of deep space,
Nothing is light, but the sun's face.
Faster than lightning, as we go,
The stars and planets are a cosmic show.

I could stare for ages at the sights
And the different coloured lights.
I'll come again one day,
Then I might stay.

James Butler (11)
Darley Dale Primary School

WAKING WOOD

Waking up on the dark wood's floor,
Wanting to be home more and more.
Leaves swishing and swashing in the air,
Lifting up my dark brown hair.
Birds of the black flying tree upon tree,
With their red gleaming eyes all staring at me.
'I'm hungry and weak' I told them so,
Please give me food or at least let me go.
Could someone be here with me, together?
I knew I was trapped here forever and ever.
As the days and weeks went by,
Sitting in the wood, asking them why?
Thinking of home,
To me now unknown.
A small door opened bright;
But to the animals of the wood it was a fright.
It took me into a shacking room . . .
Travelling through I thought I was doomed!
Footsteps I heard upon the floor,
Turning through another door,
Shadowy sulky shiny floor,
'No life for me' walking through time,
Just a big secret, definitely mine!

Lauren Eaton (10)
Darley Dale Primary School

TRANSPORT TRAIN

This is a train that goes all around the world,
Rides on every track, straight, bent and curled,
The train explores the stars, sun and moon,
To see if caterpillars are in their cocoons;
Soon there's a phone call telling him to
Relax in the blazing ball and yell, 'Chu! Chu!'
Then appears a rocket with a familiar face
And on the point, tying his lace,
Suddenly a *zoom* and an accident *chu!*
To tell you who it was, a train that says *chu* not *cuckoo!*
Soon three lorries rushed through space,
One with a mouth, one with a nose and one with two eyes which made a
face,
'Chu!' said a voice and guess who it was? A train with a face
And in his hand a massive case.
Look there's an aeroplane in a lot of pain,
It starts dropping down
Into a town,
But soon disappears and yells, 'Chu! Chu!'
Then turns into a car,
And soon drops from space and lands next to a chocolate bar;
Suddenly the car skids
And acts like a kid;
The next thing he knew he was speeding,
As fast as a cheetah that was leading,
Turned back into the train
And soon got the name the Transport Train.

Luke Jackson (10)
Darley Dale Primary School

EVERYWHERE

I'm going to space to see the stars,
The ice cream planet, to land on Mars.
I'll try my best to see the red spot,
I don't know how, it'll take a lot;
Just fancy being light years away,
If I get lost I'll come back, next day!
I'm going to climb Mount Everest,
It'll be just like passing the examiner's test.
I'll build a snowman, tall and wide,
Where I'll build it, I'll have to decide.
I'd come back soon enough anyway,
Then I'll go again! What do you say?
I think when I'm back I'll swim the Channel,
I'd be clean without using a scratchy flannel.
I'll have a small boat rowing beside me,
I just can't wait to swim in the sea!
I'll come back alive I promise I will,
Just don't keep looking from our cold window sill.
After that I'll go in a submarine,
Just think of all the things I'll have seen.
I'll try to get a mother of pearl,
When I come home it'll make your hair curl.
Now don't start crying like that,
You know you can buy a black and white cat,
I just can't help going!

Bridie Lester (11)
Darley Dale Primary School

UNDER THE SEA

Under the deep blue sea,
Looking for something I can't see.
Deeper and deeper, but only a broken ship,
And inside it was an absolute tip.
Slimy squid, crackling crabs, wonkey wood,
Nothing that was useful at all.
But then I found something amazing,
It was a great big shiny pearl
Which sent me in a whirl.
I could not believe my eyes,
It gave me such a surprise.
I picked it up and it shined a sparkling shine
Because it's way better than a boring old pine.
But now I'll have to go for now,
I have found what I was looking for.

Sarah Renwick (11)
Darley Dale Primary School

A SPACE TRIP

Blasting off to outer space,
Taking my black briefcase.
On the way we passed the moon,
I hope we will land there soon.
I pass the stars on the way
And I might land there in May.
Shooting past the planet Mars,
But not the same as chocolate bars.
The planets of different shades,
Some are smooth and some have blades.
There are 9 planets in space,
It's a shame they do not race.

Sean Pritty (10)
Darley Dale Primary School

WE'RE GOING INTO SPACE

We're going into space,
It's for the human race.
We're going to the moon,
We're going to be there soon.
We're going off to Mars
And to examine all the stars.
We'll soon be out of sight,
To see the stars shine bright.
We're going into space and we might
Go and see a satellite!
We're going to be there soon
And we'll go out with a blast! A bang!
And a boom!

Callum Kilburn (10)
Darley Dale Primary School

GOO-GAA GOO-GAA!

She looks around her lovely home,
She peers into the yard and sees a garden gnome,
This way and that way she stares and sees,
How she would love to play beneath the trees.
She falls off her behind onto knees and hands,
With one big push, she bends and stands,
Goo-gaa! Goo-gaa! I'm walking! I'm walking!
In her usual way, her baby talking,
She would do this, she would go to the shop,
You know the ones where cans always drop.
She went round aisle after aisle,
But to her it seemed like miles and miles.

Robert Wayne (11)
Darley Dale Primary School

A BOAT TRIP

For Christmas I got a brand new boat
I wanted to see if it would float.
I took it all the way to sea,
To see if it would work for me.
I found out that it could fly
And took it up extremely high.
Whizzing past the clouds and moon,
Some people were watching a cartoon.
Now I am mega high,
Flying right up in the sky.
I do not dare to look down,
Just in case I lose my crown.
Now my journey comes to an end,
Just as it started, it was my friend.

Ben Twyford (10)
Darley Dale Primary School

SPACE!

Up in the rocket, here we go
Planet to planet, we've landed, wo!
On the moon, almost flying,
Getting thirstier and thirstier,
We're almost dying.
Mars to Venus and Venus to Mars,
Up to Pluto and down to the stars.
Back down to Earth, we're all very sad,
But we'll be back again next time without our dad.

Jenny Briddon (10)
Darley Dale Primary School

THROUGH THE CLOUDS

1, 2, 3 go!
Through the clouds high and low,
To win the race
And solve the case.
To win the rest
And be the best!
At flying in my spaceship in the sky,
Past the moon high and high.
Over Mars,
I can see the stars.
Whizzing past,
I won't come last!
Jupiter's next,
What about the rest?
See the line
And the sign,
I've won!

Joanne Baldock (10)
Darley Dale Primary School

THE SUN

Brightly shining, the sun sits there in the sky,
We all don't know why.
The sun has a big shine,
It is extremely divine,
It shines down on grass,
Sometimes it melts glass.
In the morning it shines brightly,
In the day it shines silently.

Tom Dakin (11)
Darley Dale Primary School

THE FIRST AND LAST TRAIN RIDE

I clambered on the beast, it started fast,
It looked like a raging bull from the front,
As the hours went past,
It was rocking from side to side,
I couldn't stand this awful ride.

Suddenly the train rushed to a halt,
I wasn't looking,
It was a technical fault,
It was a nightmare come true,
Wouldn't you be scared if it was you?

I felt like I was welded to my seat,
I didn't know why,
I had my mum's firm grip on my feet,
We clambered off the wrecked train,
I trudged down the road but at least I had a brain.

Simon Wildgoose (10)
Darley Dale Primary School

SPACE RACE

5, 4, 3, 2, 1 blast-off!
I went into space,
To see if I could win the race,
Up, down, left, right, who knows which way is right?
People are passing me like snakes,
Colours fly past, some are green, some are red, seems to be quite clean,
I'd better go faster or I'm going to lose the race.

Matthew Dutton (10)
Darley Dale Primary School

TRAVEL TO SPACE

Fly above everything,
Higher and higher this machine goes,
Past Mercury, Venus and Mars
And then there is no gravity for my toes.

I fly around the universe,
Exploring the giant space,
With planets all around me,
To get there first is a race.

To explore every planet
And things that are below,
To find if things are living
And travel to different worlds.

Emma Boden (10)
Darley Dale Primary School

SPACE!

The ship is flying up above,
Where the stars are bright,
And it's always night.
Everything's floating upside down,
Everything's quiet.
But Earth's a riot!
Up in space it's really peaceful,
Where the stars glisten
And the moon listens.
I wish Earth could be like space,
With no wars or fights,
But it's never light.

Jenny Benyon (10)
Darley Dale Primary School

GOOD AND BAD THINGS

Go through the graveyard,
The dark and gloomy graveyard.
Go through the haunted house,
The gloomy, gloomy haunted house.
Go through the woods at night,
The scary, gloomy haunted wood at night.
Go to the scariest place in the world
School!

Ashley Hall (10)
Darley Dale Primary School

KEEPING CALM

I am blowing up inside,
Like a great big balloon
About to burst.

But on the outside I am as calm
As a mill pond,
As cool as ice.

Names drilling into my head,
Causing great pain inside,
Deep down beneath my skin is where it hurts.

They will stop soon,
Get bored and go away,
Go and torture someone else.

Keeping calm, that's the key,
To get rid of those big bad bullies,
The people who need to hurt other people to have some fun.

Charlotte Harris (11)
Furness Vale Primary School

My Nanna's Dog

My nanna's dog,
Is as daft as a frog.

She dances round the room,
Like a big baboon.

She's as black as soot
And likes a good hair cut.

She scoffs her food,
Being very rude.

Her breath is smelly,
Like an old welly.

That's my nanna's dog, Ellie,
She's got a big belly.

Joseph Perkins (10)
Furness Vale Primary School

The Bullying Rap

When you're down in the dumps
And you're feeling quite blue,
You're covered in goosebumps,
You hide in the loo.

You're feeling so lonely
And you're feeling so sad,
It's really only,
The other person that's bad.

Olivia Taylor (10)
Furness Vale Primary School

BIG BAD BULLY

Bullies are big and bad,
Inside they are soft and probably like teddies,
Grizzly and mean, nasty, snappy and bossy.

Big bad bullies are harmful and snide,
And always finding someone to pick on,
Dangerous and evil, unkind.

Bullies are a nuisance always finding something to wreck,
Unkind like an angry bear,
Lurking around,
Like a big nasty electric box,
You know how you are.

Kimberley Proctor (11)
Furness Vale Primary School

FRIENDS NOT FRIENDS

I play with someone one day,
The next with someone else,
Then in some strange way
Jealousy broke out.

We were arguing between us,
Which made me quite sad,
Now I feel I have no friends
And my friends are very glad.

Melanie Schatynski (11)
Furness Vale Primary School

RESPECT

Respect me for who I am,
Respect me for the person I am.
The colour of skin,
It's what's deep within
That counts, respect.

Respect me for the life I lead,
Respect me for the things I like.
The clothes I wear,
The things I share
Means nothing, respect.

Refrain from saying it,
Refrain from doing it,
Four eyes, goggle eyes, pie eyes too,
Blackie, paki, wackie you,
The names you call me, respect.

Refrain from laughing,
Refrain from cornering,
The fights you've caused,
The lives you've paused,
The hurt, think.

Stephanie Oldfield (11)
Furness Vale Primary School

TEACHERS!

At night when the lights are out, where do the teachers creep about?
Do they wash their socks? Do they drink lots of wine?
Do they live in houses, or do they stay at school?
Do they snore? Do they play sports?
Well, I'll follow one home tonight and then I might find out.

Rachel Spark (10)
Granby Junior School

FLORIDA

Florida is my favourite place
It is a small part of the United States
You can shop all day, from early till late
With a snack to eat, the choice is great
Hot dogs, burgers, fries and steak
All washed down with a big milkshake

Florida skies are usually sunny and blue
But around the corner lurks bad weather too
Tropical downpours, hurricanes and lightning
Sometimes fun but a little bit frightening
Gators and snakes have always lived here
So when in the swamps steer well clear

We're off to the theme parks, hip hip hooray
Where Minnie and Mickey are waiting to play
A high mountain log flume, a runaway train
Test track at Epcot now that will blow your brain
A haunted mansion, a haunted hotel
They're really scary but don't let it show

As darkness falls, look up at the sky
As large booming fireworks light up the sky
Below the umbrellas of red, blue and green
Stands a magical castle, a sight to be seen.

The Kennedy Space Centre is the place to be
Where rockets blast off, it's great to see
Up to the moon astronauts go
Out of this world, a spectacular show
This is a poem I hope you agree
Florida is great, the place for me.

Kimberley Statham (10)
Granby Junior School

UP ABOVE

Up
in the sky shining
bright,
in the
gloom of
the night,
is the
moon so
very light,
flying like a
kite.

Very
high up
above stars hover
they are a lovely
golden colour,
also a
colour yellow,
or the colour of
a marshmallow.

All
the planets
all are round,
but don't really
make much sound.
Most named after a god
or a goddess,
but they don't
look like a
mess.

Emma-Louise Fletcher (9)
Granby Junior School

THE HAUNTED HOUSE

One night
One silent night
One silent night in a spooky house
I heard a mouse creeping
I heard a mouse creeping in a silent house
Then
The wind blew hard and howled loud
The moon was clear without a cloud
Then I heard it, I jumped out, it fell with a bound
Jumped up a monster from the deep
I went as white as a sheep
I ran fast and hard then
Crash, I fell
The bang was hard, it was his perfect chance
Then, then!
I awoke in my bed
'Where is that monster?' I said.

Charlotte Cruise (9)
Granby Junior School

VALENTINE

Valentine so nice and sweet
Birds make a little tweet
Buy your girlfriend a card
And she might just take you to the park
Kiss your woman on the cheek
Because your woman smells so sweet.

Charlotte Stead (10)
Granby Junior School

ALIENS

Aliens, aliens chasing after me
Aliens, aliens trying to drink my tea
I don't like aliens, they try to eat you
You wouldn't want to know how they treat you too!
Aahh, they've got me, they've really really got me
They're going to eat me, help
I'm that scared I start to yelp
'It's OK' my mother said
'It's only a dream, now go to bed'
I don't believe her, I think it's true
I do really, I really really do
So off I go back to sleep
And that dream, my brains wants to keep.

Laura Sloman (8)
Granby Junior School

THE MAN FROM DUNDEE!

There was an old man from Dundee,
Who decided he'd have a cup of tea,
He said to his mother,
'Where the hell is my brother?
Because I've just been stung by his bee!'
Then my mother said,
'Was it down below, or on the head?'
And so I replied,
'Right there, on my thigh!'
'Look I've baked you a pie!'
And then I said, 'Mother, goodbye!'

Tanya Bridget Poole (10)
Granby Junior School

FISHES

Fishes in the water
Fishes in the sea
Captain Birdseye fetch me one for tea

Fishes in the water
Fishes in the sea
When will all this pollution cease
So they can swim free

Oil spillages here
Toxic dumping there
Poor, poor fish, soon won't be on my dish

So please look after our seas or else
There will be no more fish for us to see.

Fiona Stanley (11)
Granby Junior School

THE WINTER NIGHTS

The winter nights are long and dark,
After school no playing in the park.
The rain, wind, sleet and snow,
It is off to home I go.
Time to get changed, wash my hands,
Eat my tea, all my pets are waiting for me.
Change my rabbit's water, fill his dish,
Now it's time to feed my fish.
At last it is time for me,
Television, videos, music and my PC.
'Nicola,' my mum has said, 'it's 9 o'clock
So off to bed.'
'Goodnight.'

Nicola Manaton (9)
Granby Junior School

MY SISTER

My sister
Thinks she's a mister,
She wants a beard,
She's dead weird.

She has square glasses,
She has masses
And masses
Of thick black eyelashes.

She has action men,
She calls them Ben
Or Ken,
She even has an action man pen.

She has flat shoes,
Which goes to prove,
She wants a beard,
She's dead weird!

Lauren Barkes (10)
Granby Junior School

CRAZY JOJO

Crazy Jojo
has no brain,
crazy Jojo
has gone insane.

Crazy Jojo
is my best, funniest, mad mate,
crazy Jojo
smashed my brown plate.

Amy Doherty (10)
Granby Junior School

RABBITS!

Rabbits, rabbits everywhere,
Rabbits, rabbits all so fair,
They jump around and wave their hair,
Rabbits, rabbits so cool and rare.

My rabbit's name is Tessie,
She is so messy,
I always get the blame,
You always hear my name,
Eleanor, Eleanor sort out Tessie,
Eleanor, Eleanor she is so messy.

Wild rabbits,
Mild rabbits,
They all have bad habits.

Eleanor Hardy (11)
Granby Junior School

SUMMER DAYS

I run with the ball,
I want to win,
He trips me up and I start laughing,
I am always happy when I play with my dad.

When you hit the shuttlecock, it goes up in the air,
Sometimes it goes on the roof,
We are always laughing when we play badminton,
Lindy pretends we are at Wimbledon
And shouts the scores.

Stephen Yau (9)
Granby Junior School

SPLAT!

There was a young boy called Jack
Who played on the railway track
When a train came along he knew he was wrong
But too late! He went splat on his back!

He lay on the line
For a very long time
As if, to the track, he was bound
He looked to the right and his arms came in sight
But his legs just couldn't be found.

He screamed, so he thought, he struggled and fought
But in truth he lay there quite still
With a tear in his eye he knew he would die
Without time even to finish his will!

When he awoke (it was a dream you see, folk!)
He jumped up and down with glee
Never again will I play with a train
I'll stick to the park - that's for me!

Elizabeth Thornley (8)
Granby Junior School

FLOSS

Floss is my rabbit
She's got some bad habits
She's a bully to Nibbles
And does not care where she tiddles
She hates going back in her hutch
But we all still love her so very much.

Joanne Priest (9)
Granby Junior School

SPACE

Have you ever seen Saturn?
It may have a pretty pattern.

Have you ever seen Mars?
You'll never get there in your cars.

Have you ever seen the sun?
It may be as fat as your mum.

Have you ever seen the moon?
It may be as big as Neptune.

Have you ever seen the Milky Way?
Ev ev ev ev everyday.

Have you ever seen Pluto?
It may have a board game Subbuteo.

Have you ever seen a star?
It may be saying blah blah blah.

Have you ever seen the Earth?
How much do you think it's worth?

Matthew Dart (9)
Grassmoor Primary School

LOVE

L   is for love letters sent by an admirer
O   is for obeying the love rules
V   is for Valentine, if you're lucky
E   is for engaged to the two lovebirds.

Callum Milne (10)
Grassmoor Primary School

STORM AT SEA

The calm blue sea is a restful place,
Its gentle waves and salty breath,
Create a feeling of well-being;
Of joy at being in this human race.

When growing winds disturb the way,
And clouds appear where there were none;
I sense no humour in the rumour,
That storms will come to spoil my day.

Indeed I do not have to wonder
How long before my peace is gone;
A burst of rain. Oh what a pain!
Flashes of light, big bangs of thunder.

Stephanie Smith (10)
Grassmoor Primary School

CHRISTMAS

C   is for crackers that you pull at the dinner table
H   is for holly that hangs up high
R   is for Rudolf the red nosed reindeer
I   is for icing that decorates the cake
S   is for Santa that brings us all our prezzies
T   is for tinsel that decorates the tree
M   is for mistletoe that has a sense of romance
A   is for apple sauce you have with your Christmas dinner
S   is for surprises that are under the tree.

Kelly Oliver (10)
Grassmoor Primary School

A BEGINNER'S GUIDE TO KIDS

A   is for Ashleigh who makes lots of noise
B   is for Bradley who breaks all his toys
C   is for Cassandra who chews her toe nails
D   is for Daniel who loves to suck snails
E   is for Emma who thumps people in the face
F   is Frankie who is such a disgrace
G   is for Georgina who likes to throw stones
H   is for Harry who steals mobile phones
I   is for Imogen who will not be fed
J   is for Jack who won't sleep in his bed
K   is for Kerry who makes dirty sounds
L   is for Luke who steals hundreds of pounds
M   is for Mandy who is very unkind
N   is for Nathan who creeps up from behind
O   is for Olivia who pulls funny faces
P   is for Paul who won't tie his shoe laces
Q   is for Quintella who likes to squash ants
R   is for Richard who won't change his pants
S   is for Sadie who picks her big nose
T   is for Terry who sucks his smelly toes
U   is for Una who likes to eat slugs
V   is for Vicram who puts snails in the mugs
W is for Winnie who screams and wails
X   is for Xenos who pulls pony tails
Y   is for Yasmin who doesn't do as she should
And
Z   is for Zane who is extremely good!

Rebecca Pickering (9)
Grassmoor Primary School

WONDERFUL WINTRY WORLD

As I stepped out of my little red boat
All the snow I saw a float.

My fingers felt like I had frostbite
Everywhere you look is a magical white.

White, white, wonderful white world
The snowflakes are being twirled.

There was never seen, a polar bear
I could see my breath in the air.

All that was sparkling was all the white snow
Watching it falling as I go.

The most I could see was magical ice
That's why winter is ever so nice.

Amy Lawrence (11)
Grassmoor Primary School

AEROPLANE

An aeroplane flies very high, very high
Up in the sky very high, very high
Don't look down it's very high, very high
But when you get there you will take a sigh
And remember the good times you have when
You fly very high, very high.

Laura Ellis (11)
Grassmoor Primary School

VALENTINE

V   is for Valentine
A   is for an amazing card
L   is for the love you feel
E   is for the extremely romantic day
N   is for a night you'll never forget
T   is for a tired heart if you're let down
I   is for the night I had
N   is for the love that never breaks
E   is for every moment I'm with him.

Emma Hewitt (10)
Grassmoor Primary School

EASTER EXCITEMENT

E   is for excitement on Easter day early
A   is for assortments of different types of Easter eggs.
S   is for surprised faces when children find eggs.
T   is for trees where you hide the surprises.
E   is for eggs that the lucky people get.
R   is for the rabbit that brings all of the excitement!

Claire Walker (11)
Grassmoor Primary School

OUT OF THE WINDOW

Out of the window I can see,
Lots of friends waiting for me.
Out of the window I can see,
Lots of people in cars looking at me.
Out of the window I can see,
Children playing in the street.
Out of the window I can see,
Plants and animals which belong to me.
Out of the window I can see,
Houses across the road to me.
Out of the window I can see,
The park, the play area, where I'd like to be.
    It's just a pity I'm grounded.

Ashley Abbey (10)
Hilton Primary School

MY HAMSTER

My hamster is cute, she's as cuddly as can be
She spins in her wheel and runs up and down the bars all night long.

She eats in her bed in the morning
She is very nosey when someone comes in the room
Where her cage is.

She makes a loud noise when she's in her wheel
As she goes spinning and spinning
But she's gentle really.

Alyson Fountain (11)
Hilton Primary School

SISTER

My sister is horrible,
She's really a spoilt brat!
She goes horse riding and gets loads of presents,
(I'd rather have a pet rat!)

She gets everything she wants,
While I get nothing at all!
She blames me for everything,
Even for calling *her* small!

She winds me up to the limit,
And I never get time to myself.
She's two years younger than me,
Although she acts like her last birthday was her twelfth!

Her real name is 'Tegan'
Her initials are TEA
But why she hasn't been drunk yet,
Really puzzles me!

Her habits are disgusting,
I wouldn't be surprised if she ate glue!
I never want another one,
Definitely not two!

Rhiann Andrew (10)
Hilton Primary School

TONY ADAMS

Tony Adams is very tall
On the line heading the ball
Not very often he scores a goal
Young no he isn't, but not very old.

Arsenal is the team he plays for.
David Seaman is his teammate.
Alarming all the defenders
Making sure they don't concede a goal
Still playing football at nearly forty years old.

William Thompson (10)
Hilton Primary School

FORMULA 1

The Formula 1 cars zoom round the track
At speeds that are really fast.
But there's a car going really slow,
And he's the one that's the last!

The tyres on the car are usually grooved,
But when it's dry, they use slicks,
Without tyres the car wouldn't move,
And with them the car will be quick.

The drivers are going quite slowly,
Because it's raining and the track is wet,
And suddenly the sun starts to shine,
Then the drivers begin to sweat!

The tank is running out of petrol,
So now it will be time to pit,
But some cars won't be able to be fixed,
And then the driver has to quit!

Near the end of the race someone does an overtake,
Then they home in for the win,
And the race is won,
So the ten points they wanted are in!

Callum Argyle (11)
Hilton Primary School

PIRATES

Pirates act like they come from hell,
They probably don't even wear gel,
They ride an old dirty ship,
And they never ever drink in sips.

They each have a silver sword
But they probably get really bored
They have to put up a big sail
But really are as slow as a snail.

The evil pirate Blackbeard
But I would say he's really weird.
Long John Silver sleeps in a rotten old bed
And he really sleeps like he is dead.

When they get to some land,
They probably need a sweat band.
The captain sends them up to the crow's nest,
But everybody knows pirates are pests!

Josh Bowater (10)
Hilton Primary School

MY LITTLE COUSIN

My little cousin
Loves eating sweets
When I go to see him
He has smelly feet!

My little cousin
Loves watching TV
When I go to see him
He pays no attention to me!

My little cousin
Is only five
When I go to see him
He jumps and jives!

My little cousin
Likes playing games
When I go to see him
He's always a pain!

Alex Beech (10)
Hilton Primary School

SWIMMING POOL

Children jumping, diving, swimming,
In the pool the waters brimming.
Around the pool, swimming stars,
They can swim to planet Mars.

Underneath the water they go,
Up they rise, the bubbles they blow.
A hoop is what they can swim through.
It's amazing the things they do.

Swimming around,
Reaching the ground,
Touching the wall,
Doing front crawl.

Holding a float,
Or the inflatable boat.
The floating ring,
Or just swimming.

Alice Autrey (10)
Hilton Primary School

THE CLASSROOM

Some classrooms are old
Yet some are cold
But ours is super cold.

Some are huge
Some are slim
But ours is super cold.

The wood in some is like a century old rack
Personally I think some look like a shack
But ours is super cold.

Some are red, some are green
Few are even black or even blue
But ours is super cold.

Some have white boards
Some have black
But ours is super cold.

We shiver in it
We quiver in it
But ours is super cold!

Shaune Hill (10)
Hilton Primary School

ANOTHER BABY

I have a family of four
But I ask my mum for just one more
I don't care if it's a girl or boy
Either one I'd jump for joy.

They might be a pain
They might drive me insane
But we'd play in the sun
And have good fun.

I don't care if it's up all night
When it cries I'll hold it tight.
My mum says she's not having another baby
I just turn round and say 'Well maybe.'

Lucy Dickinson (10)
Hilton Primary School

Winter Wonderland

As I looked across the town,
The snow kept falling down and down,
And as I looked across the roof tops,
Snow on them, they looked like floor mops!

As I went out to play,
Hoping the snow wouldn't go away,
Wrapped up warm and ready to sledge,
I just hoped I wouldn't go in the hedge!

When I went to build a snowman,
Putting dry gloves on as I ran,
After I built my snowman bigger than a gnome,
Cold and wet I went back home.

When I woke up the next day,
All the snow had gone away.
But standing happily in the meadow,
Was my snowman, he's better than snow!

Summer arrives, the sun comes out,
Winter's gone, the flowers sprout.
But it's not long and I can't wait,
Winter will come, and it's never late!

Amie Broadhurst (11)
Hilton Primary School

PENGUINS

Those hairless creatures who live by the sea,
I wonder if they have sausages for tea.

Those black and white animals they wobble
                                    like jelly,
I wonder if they have sky digital on the telly.

Those goggle eyed creatures they look a bit funny,
I wonder if they have a pet fluffy bunny.

Those flappy black wings by their sides,
I wonder if they go down water slides.

Those funky little black dudes they're rolling all over the place,
I wonder if they go on holiday they pack fish in their suitcase.

Henri Dare (10)
Hilton Primary School

MY PET RABBITS

I've got rabbits, lots of them too,
They sit in their hutch all day long,
Then I come with a scoop full of corn,
And they bounce around the hutch full of glee.

Some of them are fat, some of them are skinny,
It makes no odds to me,
I like them all the same.
Some of them are hairy,
Some have short hair,
But I still love them all the same.

Cheryl Beech (11)
Hilton Primary School

HOMEWORK!

Homework, homework, it's one thing I hate,
If I dare I'll hand it in late.
There's one person I know, that's my mate.

Homework, homework, I'd scribble you up,
but then I won't get a new pup.
And when I've finished I'll want a drink in my new cup.

Homework, homework, I sometimes like you
But sometimes I get mad and I say,
'I don't want it but who does?'

Homework, homework, I hate you I do.
Who wants you I don't know just who.
I hate you!

Holly Frost (11)
Hilton Primary School

FOOTBALLER

David Beckham on the run,
John Motson having some fun,
Michael Owen making a pass,
Andy Cole tripping on the wet grass.
In the World Cup when England played France,
Roy Keane started to dance,
Giggs! Scoring a great goal,
Dennis Wise did a forwards roll!
Paul Scholes with the volley,
Dwight Yorke is feeling jolly,
Teddy Sheringham with a great hit,
Ninety minutes was up and that was it!

Jordan Peck (10)
Hilton Primary School

MAGGIE

Maggie is my pet dog,
She's very boisterous and likes to go on walks a lot.
Another one of her favourite things is food
She gets that as long as she's good.
Sometimes she can be naughty and bad,
So she lies in her bed and looks all sad!
She can always be really funny,
Like when she goes to sniff at my pet bunny!
When you say 'Now where's that food I saw?'
Straight away she'll give you her paw.
With her big brown eyes,
At the cheeky cat next door she spies.
Also she likes care, attention and love,
But most especially great big hugs!
As a present she offers you her orange blanket,
All you can say is 'Oh thank you.'
My mum often calls her a baddie.
But that's OK, that's my
        Maggie!

Bethan Jones (10)
Hilton Primary School

HOMEWORK!

Homework is very bad,
It really makes me very sad.
At forty nine Back Lane,
I'm told I am a real pain.

If I don't give it in on time
My teacher will begin to whine
So I avoid the teacher for the rest of the day,
And if she forgets I shout hooray.

So far this week she hasn't remembered,
Because of the excuses I have invented.
So children, homework's bad,
Don't do it because it makes you sad!

Thomas Land (11)
Hilton Primary School

THE OLD DAY TOONS

Remember the times of Hong Kong Phooey
Of Top Cat and Scooby Doo?

Remember the time of those Flintstones who were
Best Friends with the well known Rubbles.

The fluffy wuffy Bagpuss on the table who's
Making a come back as the babies wail.

Remember those Wacky races with danger
Lurking in every lay-by?

Remember Blue Peter and the funky old music
The mad men presenters and the crazy trips?

Remember the dastardly Dick Dastardly
Trying to catch the pigeon
With his canine laughing friend Mutley.

So, with all the excitement,
Remember these programmes time is over,
And back into storage they'll go
But hey, they'll always live on in your parents minds.

Jack Wall (11)
Hilton Primary School

MY TWIN

My twin he's a right pain
He gets on my nerves like mad
He always tells everybody my secrets
Being a twin's really really bad.

He always switches over TV channels
Especially when I'm watching them
He kicks me, punches me and pulls my ears
So I'm forced to tell on him.

He's broken nearly all my models
And he always sets my alarm clock to six in the morning
It rings and rings and rings
So I get up and start yawning.

At school he hates maths the same as me
In science we're doing about weight and mass
In his group he's doing about nature
Thank goodness I'm in the other class.

My twin he's a right pain
But I suppose as he's my twin, I must be the same.

Greg Purnell (11)
Hilton Primary School

ALIENS

In the future they might come and land
But their language we won't understand.
Will they be green with pink fluffy spots
Or eyes of plenty, lots and lots?

Will they bring peace or war
Will they have the same rules and law?
They might be the same size as us
Or be the size of a double-decker bus.

Will they be big and scary
Or maybe small and hairy?
Are they from the planet Mars
Did they come in funny looking cars?

James Purnell (11)
Hilton Primary School

MY LITTLE SISTER

My little sister's really cheeky,
My little sister's really loud,
My little sister thinks she's the funniest,
My little sister is always playing dollies.

My little sister's greedy,
My little sister doesn't share,
My little sister hogs all the chocolates,
My little sister thinks she's the best.

My little sister's in year one,
My little sister's only five.
My little sister's birthday is August 21st when she'll be six.
My little sister always plays.

My little sister has long blonde hair,
My little sister has dark blue eyes,
My little sister has freckles dotted on her nose,
My little sister has pale skin.
    My little sister's adventurous!

Helen Roddis (11)
Hilton Primary School

MY FAVOURITE ANIMALS

My favourite animals are all very sweet
especially the cute budgie that goes tweet, tweet!

My favourite animals like eating grass
when we're in the car it's horses we pass!

My favourite animals live in cages
they are hamsters, they live for ages!

My favourite animals live in the sea
whales and dolphins that look up at me

My favourite animals can be very loud
dogs with pointy teeth running along the ground!

My favourite animals are very big hoppers
rabbits have two sharp teeth and use their choppers!

These are my favourite animals I haven't got just one
because they are all jumpy and cute they are all so much fun.

Genna Tooley (11)
Hilton Primary School

BUILDINGS

B   uildings are big, buildings are small
U   nder the ground they are not very tall
I   n towns and cities they can reach giant heights
L   arge buildings have lots of lights
D   ingy buildings, buildings are all about.
I   nside buildings are often bright coloured
N   ever has a building been put where sand is under foot
G   round is often soft that's where a foundation is put.
S   ometimes buildings are blown to the ground by tornadoes.

Jason Whitworth (11)
Hilton Primary School

MY SISTER!

In the mornings I'm fast asleep
I'm lying in my bed.
Oh what a surprise to see,
Her sitting by my head.

It doesn't matter where I am,
Apart from being at school.
She follows me absolutely everywhere,
And totally acts like a fool.

She pinches all my chocolates,
I think that's really bad.
She gets me into trouble,
She's really, really mad!

Ian Richards (10)
Hilton Primary School

MY SISTER

My sister has short hair and glasses,
And a big cheeky grin like she's up to something,
She has tiny toes,
Ears, fingers, mouth and nose.
She is special, she can be sweet,
She goes to the hospital once a week.
She likes chip butties and play in footie
And getting muddy.
She likes boys with lots of toys and a PlayStation too,
Her favourite colour is blue.

Beth Wilson (11)
Hilton Primary School

I WISH I HAD A SISTER

I wish I had a sister,
If I had a sister I'd love her lots and lots,
If I had a sister she'd share her room with me,
If I had a sister I'd name her Bethany.

I wish I had a sister,
Brothers are a pain, they're worse than sisters,
My mum would love another baby,
But Dad just couldn't take another one.

I wish I had a sister,
My friends would love her so,
I wish I had a sister,
I would always help to care for her.

I wish I had a sister!

Carrie-Ann Hollands (10)
Hilton Primary School

MY BROTHER

I have a little brother
He doesn't get on with his mother
He gets on with his dad
Unless he has been bad.

My brother is a pain
He really is quite vain
Sometimes we are friends
But it usually ends.

Sometimes when I'm bored
I say let's play with that sword
But then I call him names
He says not now James.

James Wood (10)
Hilton Primary School

TELEVISION

I love sitting in front of the screen
Watching skinny actors perform their scene
Some films are funny, some films are sad,
Most films are good but some can be bad.

Take some war films in black and white
Then watch a horror film which will give you a fright.
Comedy films are funny they make me laugh,
Education films are boring but they teach you maths.

TV can be good but not too much
You can't always sit in front of the TV watching Frank and Butch,
Go and play out or read in your room
'Cause you don't want to end up a couch potato baboon.

Kim Shawcross (11)
Hilton Primary School

BROTHERS

Some brothers are good,
Some brothers are bad,
Some tease you,
Some make you sad.

But some brothers are kind,
They're hard to find.
And some brothers are potty
They really drive you dotty.

Some brothers are skinny,
Some brothers are fat,
Though brothers are strange things really,
I love my brother dearly!

Sarah Lawton (10)
Hilton Primary School

SCHOOL

Why is school so boring, as boring as a buzzing bee?
Why was it made for people like you and me?

My worst subject is geography, it really, really bores me
But then again I don't like RE.

Why is art the best, better than all the rest?
But I get in such a terrible mess.
At the end I just have to take a guess.

Why, please tell me, why school is so
boring?

Emily Wheildon (10)
Hilton Primary School

FLUFFY WUFFY

Fluffy wuffy
Black and white
There's a dog
Flying by.

Fluffy wuffy
Black and white
Do you think
He's going to bite?

Fluffy wuffy
Soft and round
When he barks
I love the sound.

Anthony Durose (10)
Ilam CE Primary School

DEEP DOWN

Deep down underground
Criss cross they end up to one big stone wall
Oh hungry, hungry got no one here to help me
Suddenly it's opening up
Woh there's a lorry taking . . .
What are they
Chips?
Deep down underground
Cling clang pots and pans
Nan my gran fries eggs sky high in a sizzling frying pan
Deep down.

James Richardson (9)
Ilam CE Primary School

GRANDAD ARTHUR HOWSON

As my grandad crept away
I said to myself I will never
forget that day.
He used to play with my brother,
Cousin, and me in the shed . . .
But now he can't because he's dead.
I saw him dead it made me cry,
It was horrible to see him in
Pain and then die.
But it's not so bad because
I can see,
Lots of happy times in my memory.

His car is there waiting for a new owner
To drive it away,
It will be sad when we sell it
soon one day.
Now he's sadly at an end
But never mind
Because he's always in my
Heart,
Soul
and mind.

Hannah Tudor (9)
Ilam CE Primary School

PUFF PUFF GOES THE TRAIN

Puff puff goes the train
In the mist and in the rain
It rumbles by with a roar
And all the little boys shout cor!

It stops at stations and village halls
To check the train for any faults
It rumbles by with a roar
And all the little boys shout cor!

Giles Whitta (9)
Ilam CE Primary School

THE SIMPSONS

The Simpsons family are very mild
But when you meet Bart he's a terrible child
There's only one thing you can do with him
That is put him in the bin
And there's Homer he's always at the bar
And do you know he gets around
He gets around in an old pink car
And now we move on to Santa's little helper
He is always eating Homer's shoe
And always drinking water out of the loo
And not forgetting Grandpa
He's always totally bizarre.
Even if you say hello
He thinks you said I ate my toe.
And now we move on to Lisa
She is never a teaser
And there's Maggie and Marge
They loved it when they went on the barge.
And that is the Simpsons family.

Christopher Mabey (9)
Ilam CE Primary School

THE DESERTED HOUSE

Here we go down to the haunted house,
It's near my Scottish home.
Now it is very cold out there,
So I'd take a lot of care.
Before you go i-in-side,
I think you're sure of a big surprise
Cos this is where the ghosts are very scary!

There was one man that went inside,
But he never ca-ame out.
If you can see what he saw,
I think you should give a shout.
It's a very creaky house,
So I'd come in like a mouse.
Cos this is where the ghosts are very
            Scary!

(Sung to the tune of 'Teddy Bears Picnic')

Lucy Hack (10)
Ilam CE Primary School

ALL THINGS NICE

The sun is shining in the sky
I lie on the grass with glitter coming down.

Sugar and spice and everything nice
Lollipops on the grass and flowers too.

Blossom in the tree and bubbles popping high.

Clouds in the sky swaying
Like swings that you play on.

Becky Allen (8)
Loscoe CE Primary School

JOURNEY UP THE STAIRS

Up the first step 'I need a drink'
'You don't!' Mum bellowed.
On to the second step 'I need to go to the toilet'
'Get to bed' screamed Mum.
The third step next 'I've cut my hand, I need a plaster'
'Very funny' chuckled Mum!
Up to the fourth,
'I need to do my homework'
'Do it in the morning.'
Up to the eighth
'My sister's having a heart attack'
'Get to bed!'
On the tenth I gave in and went to bed.

Alex Tennant (10)
Loscoe CE Primary School

LONELY AGAIN

L   eft out
O   n your own
N   o one cares a bit
E   veryone walks away
L   onely all the time
Y   et another day.

A   girl's just walked past me
G   etting excited
A   friend or a foe
I   n luck
N   ever let go of hope.

Kirsty Holmes (10)
Loscoe CE Primary School

GOAL

I pick the ball up
running as fast as the wind
tackles from this side
and tackles from that side
I just carry on and that is that.

Just out their area
And I'm worried sick
I shouldn't worry
I never ever miss.

I'm taking my aim
to get on target
my foot goes back
with plenty of power
I strike.

The keeper goes down
but misses the ball
the ball breaks the net
    goal! goal! goal!

Ashley Mellors (9)
Loscoe CE Primary School

SPACE

I'm flying through space
Around the galaxy
Without a trace
I travel the universe.

I've travelled the Milky Way
And seen the galaxy
Standing on my docking bay
I've seen the world.

And now I must go
To travel the universe,
Discover intelligent life so
There's another race.

Gareth Summers (10)
Loscoe CE Primary School

GOING TO HOGWARTS

I start at platform nine and three quarters
To catch Hogwarts Express
Takes about one hour.

Twelve o'clock - finally got there,
Met Harry and Ron,
They take me around Hogwarts.

At night we met Hermione,
We were walking
in the forbidden forest
Suddenly, we saw Lord Voldemort.

We hid in a bush,
then he went away.
We crept out of the bush
and decided to curse a spell
on Lord Voldemort.

Sadly it didn't work
It was time to go
I caught Hogwarts Express again
And went home.

Sam Smith (8)
Loscoe CE Primary School

JOURNEY TO THE MOON

We're going up in a rocket
to find the big, round moon,
There's Saturn, Mars, Pluto, Earth,
Look the golden coin-like sun.

We're landing on the grey bold moon
It's such a pretty sight
bouncing on the moon all night
Up go our feet
into the wonderful air.

Lots of holes all around
but where is all the sound?
Put the flag in the hole
now it's time to go home.

Helen Willis (9)
Loscoe CE Primary School

MR DINO'S VOYAGE

Wide open fields full of other dinosaurs.
Then my eye catches lunch
She sees me - she starts to gallop
I decide to go and crunch
Her hard bones
I chase after her
Faster and faster I gain in my speed
When I catch her I will howl like a bear
I squash all the grass
I go for a leap
Then I catch her at long last.
Eventually the bones rot away into the ground.

David Hancock (9)
Loscoe CE Primary School

SEASONS

When spring is here the grass starts to grow
the flowers start to blossom
the butterflies flutter in the spring day.
Summer is here the days are longer
the sun is hotter,
and we get to play out longer!
It's autumn, the leaves are on the ground
as beautiful as ever.
The birds are not singing,
Does it mean that winter is here?

Winter is here at last, the spider webs
glittering in the frost.

Jade Walker (10)
Loscoe CE Primary School

GOING TO HOGWARTS

One day I went to Diagon Alley
I brought a wand, broom and books
Then on to Hogwarts I went.

At twelve o'clock I got to Hogwarts
Met Harry, Ron and Hermione.
The first thing we did
Was to put a curse on evil Voldemort.

The best time was Christmas
I got a firebolt and a jumper from Ron's mum.

Robert Hughes (9)
Loscoe CE Primary School

UP THE STAIRS TO BED

'Go to bed' said Mum.
'No' I said.
Mum said 'Go.'
Onto the first step
'Mum my programme's on'
'No!' Mum shouted.
Onto the second step
'Mum I need a drink.'
'Go to bed!' Mum screamed.
Onto the third step
'I feel sick'
'Go to bed then,' said Mum.
'You'll feel better!'
Onto the fourth step
'Can I read?'
'No' said Mum.
'Just go to bed!'
Onto the fifth, sixth, seventh, eighth step
'Mum you need to know this - my back aches!'
'I don't care!' Mum screamed.
'Just go to bed I need some peace.'
'OK then Mum you win, but next time I'll get my revenge.'

Hannah Lowe (10)
Loscoe CE Primary School

LIFE OF SUMMER

I like the moon at night and it's a pretty sight
I like the green grass, because you can lie on it
Every day at my house it smells beautiful.
There is a buzzy bee under my bed.

Charlotte Truman (9)
Loscoe CE Primary School

WALKING IN SPRING

Winter is cold
Autumn is too
Leaves are falling
King of the world
Ice when you're walking
Never warm, always cold.

Ice never in spring
Never cold as well
Spring is my favourite season
People walking like me
Racing around in the park
Sun shining as bright as it can
Now kids racing around the acorn tree
Gold spring, gold spring
Just like me.

Daniel Evans (9)
Loscoe CE Primary School

MY JOURNEY IN THE FIELDS

The sun is bright
You can hear the wind
Whistling through the trees.
The grass is like glitter
The spiders webs are silver metal
Butterflies are colourful
Then a rainbow.
The flowers are colourful than ever before,
Don't the fields look beautiful
This time of year?

Michael Quigley (10)
Loscoe CE Primary School

GOING TO BED

Up step number one
Mum 'I think I've broken my leg'
'Get to bed, now!'
Up step number two
'Mum I need a drink'
'Go to bed now!'
Up step number three
'Mum I forgot my teddy'
'Get up the wooden hill now!'
Up step number four
five, six and seven
'Mum I've got a cold'
'Get up now.'
'Mum I've got up now OK?'

Christian Rue (10)
Loscoe CE Primary School

THE MOON

I'm here the moon
The sky is pink like a pig
The trees are yellow
Houses made of maltesers
Aliens are everywhere
The grass is blue with orange spots
A school is shaped like a number five
The cars are made of red, red jelly.

Danny Allsopp (10)
Loscoe CE Primary School

LUCKY

My love, my life, my everything
My heart, my soul
My day, my night
My special little friend
Who will be there to the end
He's there for me
When I need him
He's gorgeous and kind
Forever mine.
I love him so
He will never go
He'll stay with me
And later you'll see
He's mine, my Lucky
My lucky rabbit.

Shareen Akthar (11)
Markeaton Primary School

THE TEDIOUS TEACHERS

Tedious teachers,
Go on and on,
Like a snake hissing in your ear,
Like a colony of ants ready to attack,
Tedious teachers,
Some teachers can be fun.

Joanna Turner-Attwell (9)
Markeaton Primary School

CHESTER ZOO

I like the swinging,
acrobatic chimps,
the curious babies
and their furious parents.
The noise they make will
give an earthquake,
so beware of the shake.

I like the humpy, bumpy camels,
the humps will stick out
and the bumps will wobble.

The hanging tongues,
The banging feet,
All at Chester Zoo.

Jessica Buckley (10)
Markeaton Primary School

THE BEST FRIENDS

The best friends chat and laugh
Like a pair of identical twins
It makes me feel happy
Like a colourful rainbow reflecting down on earth.

Sam Waywell (9)
Markeaton Primary School

THE FROG

The frogspawn floats
In the deep blue pond
Like lots of beady eyes
Staring, staring.

The tadpole swims
With a swish of its tail.
Like a little black fish
Whizzing, whizzing.

The frog croaks
On the lily pad
It swims the breaststroke
Gliding, gliding.

Matthew Ripley (10)
Markeaton Primary School

THE BURNING CANDLE

The flame on the candle flickers,
Up into the air.
As I watch the burning wax slither,
The flame looks at me with its cunning little glare.
The wax slithers down the side,
Just like a slow flowing waterfall.
Around the candlewick a pool of wax
grows larger,
Until the flame will burn no more.

Becky Wainwright (9)
Markeaton Primary School

FUNNY ANIMAL

A fish with angel's wings
And lives with a king.

A lion with an elephant's trunk
Ad smells like a big fat skunk.

A snake with a lion's head
And lives in a hedge.

A boy with a sheep arm
And always is so calm.

A flamingo with two metallic purple beaks
And always pecks people's cheeks.

A kangaroo with a zebra's head and tail
And always looks very pale.

A hamster with ears of a rabbit
And has a very bad habit.

Patrick Doohan (11)
Markeaton Primary School

BUZZY BEES

Buzzy bees
Buzz buzz buzz
Buzzing around everywhere
Collecting pollen from flowers
They can take hours and hours.
Bees never stop buzzing
Buzzy bees
Buzz buzz buzz.

Kate Shelton (9)
Markeaton Primary School

MY CLASS MATES

Sammy Richardson is the fastest runner,
Laura Coilway can give you a laugh,
Andrew Oxford thinks he's the best footballer,
Amanda Morse rides a horse.
Rocky Milda who picks his nose,
Sarah McKenzie can do a lot of sport,
Haydn Williams is just a complete show off,
Joanna McKenna's hair is henna.
Joshua McDonald bites his nails,
Hannah Freeman can do gymnastics,
Brad Wilson is a bit like a professor,
Becky Dale is a great tap, ballet, modern dancer.
These are all the things my class mates do.

Joanne Eaton (9)
Markeaton Primary School

DANCE

I like different dances
Some happy, some sad
My dad goes wild in rock 'n' roll.
When my mum hears a beat
She doesn't stop till the end of the week.
When my sister Phoebe
hears the Tweenie beat
She kicks her feet.
Nanny's wobbling all over the place.

Naomi Norton (8)
Markeaton Primary School

SOMETHING IN MY HOUSE

Yesterday I saw something little, it looked just like a mouse,
But it told me it was a Troud and lived in my house.
I wondered what a Troud was and what it liked to eat,
But when I asked it, it said tomato ketchup, Brussel sprouts, mixed
                                        with shredded wheat.
Yesterday I made it, it really makes me sick,
But when I gave it him he said it was a trick.
It ran around the room laughing really loud, you must be thick,
                                        I'm a mouse not a Troud,
I chased him up the stairs, I chased him up and down,
He was just as happy as a king that's just received his crown.
I never saw the mouse again but if I ever do,
I'll chase him into the bathroom and flush him down the loo.

Troud-tr-ow-d.

Katie Mackervoy (10)
Markeaton Primary School

THE DUSTY DESERT

The dusty desert
Full of golden sand
Like a jar of sweets packed to the brim.
Like a school crowded with children.
It makes me feel claustrophobic
Like a mouse stuck in a corner.
It makes me realise what a full life we lead.

Emily Burton (11)
Markeaton Primary School

GRAN'S HANDBAG

In Gran's handbag there were . . .
Flags, nags
Hags, crags
All in an old carpet bag.

There were odd things,
Odd things
Like peas in a pod.

There was a rumbling, tumbling, crumbling sound
Like an aeroplane trying to land such a kerfuffel made by
the rumble of an old ice cream van.

A football team
A big machine
A small ice cream
A middle sized bean,
Pop goes the bean, it's not been seen
Runs away today.

Hannah Baker (10)
Markeaton Primary School

WINTER TIME

In winter the snow is scattered on the grass like a silver crown.
Trees are bare, snow is falling so let's have fun before it all melts.
The cars are covered in slippery ice so adults scrape the snow off.
Kids are dressing up in warm clothes and walk outside and see their
friends and shout . . .

. . . It's winter time.

Craig Mackervoy (8)
Markeaton Primary School

THE DRAGON

The Dragon
A fire breathing monster
flying, soaring, swooping
like a great volcano bird
like a monster of the sky
a menace in my eyes
I am so small and like a mouse
or even a louse
The Dragon
a fire breathing dinosaur.

Tom Bayliss (11)
Markeaton Primary School

EVIL ALIENS

Out in space where the stars are.
There could be evil aliens.
Aliens that come down to Earth to destroy
And cast a spell on the Earth
To make people turn evil and start to hate each other.
So if you wonder one day why the world is full of fights
It could have been evil aliens
        Casting spells.

Abigail Williams (10)
Markeaton Primary School

THE BEACH

See the sea crashing on the shore,
See the fish swimming forever more.
Hear the waves splashing all day,
Hear the children as they play.
Watch the crabs scurry swiftly,
As the birds fly briskly.

Serena Jackson (11)
Markeaton Primary School

ANIMALS

Cats camouflage in the dark,
Dogs are brown as bark,
Fish are coloured like shiny gold,
Ponies as white as clouds,
Rabbits are black as coal.

Chloe Tidey (9)
Markeaton Primary School

THE DOLPHIN

The dolphin splashes in sparkling blue water
Its arched body jumping up and down
Like a see-saw on a lush green park
It makes me feel happy
Like a flying bird floating in the breeze.

Amy Waywell (11)
Markeaton Primary School

SEASONS OF THE YEAR

Spring's the time of year,
When blossom's on the trees.
Summer's the time of year
For the buzzing of the bees.
Autumn's the time of year,
for leaves floating in the breeze.
Winter's the time of year,
When all the rivers freeze.
And then it all comes round to
Spring with blossom on the trees.

Joanna Tollitt (8)
Markeaton Primary School

THE TWISTING TORNADO

The twisting tornado
One of the cruellest effects of weather
Enormous, destructive, brutal
Like a giant spinning top coming down from Heaven
Like a hoover sucking up everything around.
It makes me feel scared,
Like my life is going to end,
The twisting tornado
Reminds us how destructive life can be.

Alexander Fairlie (11)
Markeaton Primary School

THE MAGICAL SEASHELL LAND

The magical seashells sparkle in the sun,
They bring joy to more than one.
If you joyfully open one up,
You will surely have more fun.
It'll take you to a brand new place,
And you will have a spanking new face.
When you get there you will see,
More than just a boring TV.
Chocolate ice cream that's a clue,
But there is surely more to do.

Alisa Hamzic (9)
Markeaton Primary School

SKATEBOARDING

Skateboarding takes time to learn,
But it's worth it for what you earn.
Tony Hawk the most influential
He makes tricks look accidental.
Mullen Mastred the casper to 360° flip
While doing it he lost the board's grip
Elissa Steamer, Rune Glifberg to name a few,
With those people its popularity grew and grew.

Byron Day (11)
Markeaton Primary School

SNOWY DAYS

Outside in the garden, all is white and all is still.
Everything is cold and shiny.
Everyone's asleep and cosy.
In the morning everyone wakes up
To see outside is white and frozen.
All day long they play in it,
Build snowmen in the sparkling white snow.
They make little angels in the smooth snow.
At last the children with frozen hands rush inside and get warm.
Finally it's dark.
All the children look through dark windowpanes wondering
'Will it snow again?'

Rhys Jones (8)
Markeaton Primary School

SNOW

The snow-covered houses seem asleep
As the frosty wind blows.
Crystal-white snow shines in the scarlet of the lunar eclipse,
The red colour cascades upon the blanket of fluffy snow.

The eclipse darkens down and starts to fade.
The freezing night turns the powdery snow into blue-white ice.
The snow can hardly be seen.
By morning light it has turned to slushy mush
And disappears.

Alex Davidson (8)
Markeaton Primary School

SEASIDE

S andy beaches covered with multicoloured shells,
E verywhere people are lying on the beach, playing ball games
and sunbathing.
A djacent islands float in the nearby waters of the sea.
S hops bursting with holiday souvenirs.
I ced lollies licked by hungry children,
D inghies float up and down on the gentle waves,
E astern winds blow like a whispering voice, in the silent rock pools.

Lorna East (9)
Markeaton Primary School

THE TREE HOUSE

The secretive tree house
Built by me and my friends
Wooden, hidden, high
Like a hollow room, perched in a tree,
Like an eye, staring out over the town
It makes me feel safe inside its solid walls
Like a hedgehog under all its protective prickles
The secretive tree house.
And I am the king, concealed inside it.

Sarah Eley (10)
Markeaton Primary School

WINTER

All the children by the fire,
Keeping warm and safe.
Wishing they were in the snow,
Tingling their hands and face.

Now the children are in the snow,
Playing on the white hills.
Then it begins to snow again,
Giving them frosty chills.

The children make a snowman,
And a carrot for his nose.
Some tinsel for a scarf,
And ten pebbles for his toes.

The children walk back home again,
Tomorrow will it snow?
Will we be able to go and play some more?
Well I really do not know!

Natalie Bryan (8)
Markeaton Primary School

I LIKE RICE

I like rice
I like it cooked really nice
Fried in the frying pan
Grilled in the grill
Cooked in the oven
And laid on the sill.

Laura Blackwell (11)
Markeaton Primary School

A DINOSAUR

This dinosaur started life as any other dinosaur
an egg, just an ordinary egg.
After a couple of months it hatches,
it evolves into a little carnivore.

It eats slabs of meat from its mother, it plays
while its mother nests.

It grew and grew until it was twelve metres long
and strong legs to support its weight.

It's got teeth with saw like edges to bite its prey
Its jaw can hold up to 70kg of meat.

It was one of the most fierce dinosaurs to ever walk the planet.

What was the name of this monstrous creature
who lived more than 65,000,000 years ago?

Laura Gilmore (9)
Markeaton Primary School

THE NIGHT OF THE ECLIPSE

On the night of the eclipse the moon disappears,
Then turns bright red for a minute or two.
As the eclipse slowly darkens
The ice on the pond shines like five glittering stars.
The eclipse disappears
The moon comes out again
The eclipse has gone
For another century.

Oliver Wilkinson (8)
Markeaton Primary School

SNOW

Snowflakes falling one by one
Catch one in your hand,
Sparkling, glittering,
Interesting shapes
Each with a pattern of its own.

Falling, falling everywhere,
Making ground all white,
Sparkling, glittering,
Curly patterns, everywhere,
Icy shapes and swirls.

Josie Hough (9)
Markeaton Primary School

BLOSSOM

In spring you get some blossom,
As pink as it can be.
And when I walk to school,
It always falls on me,
Last night I saw some more,
I took it home with me,
And I sprinkled it in my bed,
Where I dreamt of them.

Sophie Ross (8)
Markeaton Primary School

SNOW

The sun glistens on
The fluffy snow
Crystal clear snowfaces
Fall from the pure sky.

The snow glitters
Like the stars.
Children stamp in the
Powdery snow.
The moon turns red
As night approaches.

Jake Williamson (8)
Markeaton Primary School

WINTER TIME

It's winter time at last,
The snow has fallen fast.
The snow sparkles on the ground,
There isn't a single flower to be found.
The cold wind blowing around my head
Makes my ears go red.
The trees are leafless and very still,
They're frozen stiff by Jack Frost quill.

Paloma Hinojosa (8)
Markeaton Primary School

WINTER

Winter is now here.
We have to put on our winter clothes.
Icicles frozen to the bench,
My shadow shows in the snow.
The trees are leafless and damaged
from the strong cold wind.
They are bare with a few branches
When I breathe, my cold breath wanders off in the freezing air.

Jessica Phillips (8)
Markeaton Primary School

I HAD A LITTLE GUINEA PIG

I had a little guinea pig,
Who loved to do the jig
He really loved to dance although
I never gave him chance;
He woke me in the night
And gave me such a fright
He loved to keep the beat
On his little little feet.

Robyn Browning (8)
Markeaton Primary School

WINTER

The cool wind blows as the
roads shimmer in the sun.
The cold trees leafless branches glitter
in the sunlight.
The snow on the grass is blue,
as the sun slowly warms the grass up.

Tom Thompson (8)
Markeaton Primary School

THE MIDNIGHT CRY

It was once a dark lonely night
When the clock stopped
and gave me a fright.
So I looked out my window
and started to stare
to see if anybody else was there.
So I looked at the time, twelve o'clock
I heard a scream
and a little knock.
What could it be?
Who could be there?
I didn't move
Or try to glare
Out of the window
there it stood
crying out
as hard as it could.
I opened the door
who could it be? . . .
but my little pussy cat
crying for me!

Megan Mellor (11)
Moorhead Primary School

BATS

They fly at night and give you a fright,
Swooping and screeching in the dead of night.

In the dark they fly,
Can't see with their eyes,
Nobody can hear their spooky cries,
Hunting for food, for some insects, some flies.

Fangs glow white in the dead of night,
As they suck their prey dry.
Into the night they fly.

Home as dawn breaks,
To their belfry they glide.

Resting as day comes,
Light passes them by.

Rose Akers (10)
Moorhead Primary School

BULLIES ARE BAD

Bullies are bad
They can make you sad
When pushing and shoving
Bullies are bad.

Bullies are rotten
They play with cotton
When punching and kicking
Bullies are bad.

Bullies are mean
They should never be seen
When saying horrible things
Bullies are bad.

Samantha Smith (8)
Moorhead Primary School

CLOWNS

Orange hair
Pointed hat
Big red nose
Things like that.

They chase around
The circus rings
Doing lots of
Silly things.

Squirting water
Tripping up
Teasing children
With a cup.

Blowing bubbles
Through their ears
Then you cry
With joyful tears.

The circus ends
It's time to cheer
Goodbye clowns
Until next year!

Charlotte Robinson (9)
Moorhead Primary School

LITTLE TILLY TUMBLE TREE

Little Tilly Tumble Tree sat upon a bumblebee
It stung her on the bottom,
Which made her feel quite rotten
She didn't blame the bumblebee
Because she'd sat upon his knee.
Which hurt the bee so very bad
And made poor Tilly feel so sad.
'I'm oh so sorry Mr Bee,
I didn't mean to hurt your knee'
Said Little Tilly Tumble Tree.
So if you sit upon a branch, be very careful
For by chance, there may be something resting
Like a bird that's starting nesting,
Or a beautiful butterfly fast asleep
So always look before you leap.

Simone Rochester (8)
Moorhead Primary School

PET POEM

Pets are lovely animals for instance a cuddly camel.
Maybe a dog or a slimy frog.
Furry cats or black bats.
A mole that could live in a hole.
A flea, it could live on your key.
What about a rabbit, it could be your habit.
You cold do your course on a horse.
You could have a hare you will have to take care.
What about me?

Danielle Ottewell (9)
Moorhead Primary School

142

THE LITTLE FLY AND THE BIG BEE

Flying, flying,
Through the sky.

Clouds to see,
As they are passing by.

Bees are big,
Flies are small.

Bees sting,
Flies don't.

Flies fly higher,
Bees fly lower.

Cherrelle Barley (8)
Moorhead Primary School

NETBALL

N   etball is fun to play
E   nergetic girls and boys
T   eam work is important
B   rilliant, we scored a goal!
A   lways follow the rules,
L   eading the ball to a goal
L   ong passes make you win.

Jessica Mahey (10)
Moorhead Primary School

THE DANCE EXAM

I wake up in the morning,
Full of excitement and hope.
For today it is my dance exam
Can I really cope?

In the class tension is rising,
I tie my ribbons in my shoes,
My hands are shaking, my legs like jelly,
Have I got something to lose?

I enter the room, she's waiting there,
I get in position and point my toes,
The music starts and I move my feet,
And I end it with a pose!

Katy York (10)
Moorhead Primary School

BALLS

Balls bounce up and down,
Big ones, small ones, spotty ones
and stripey ones.
Balls bounce up and down,
Like people jumping up and down.
Balls bounce up and down,
Throw them, catch them,
Bounce them and kick them.
Balls bounce up and down,
    Bounce,
        Bounce
            Bounce
                Bounce.

Holly Fowke (11)
Moorhead Primary School

COOKIES

Cookies, cookies, they're so yummy,
I store them in my tummy.
Chocolate chip,
In a milky dip,
Cookies are so scrummy.

Melissa Brentnall (11)
Moorhead Primary School

WONDERFUL, WONDERFUL SPACE

The bright, golden fiery sun,
Staring at Mercury's rocky surface,
Mercury who is staring
At Venus the planet of love,
Whilst Venus is gazing at Earth,
The only planet to have life,
Earth is peering at Mars
And its wonderful glowing red.
Mars is gaping at Jupiter,
The largest planet in the solar system,
Jupiter is staring at Saturn's spinning ring.
Saturn is now glimpsing at Uranus' grey clouds,
Uranus has the longest stare,
Staring at Neptune, god of the sea,
Neptune looking at Pluto,
Pluto, silent Pluto, small Pluto.
Wonderful, wonderful space.

Jessica Siddall (8)
Redhill Primary School

A VOYAGE IN SPACE

We are going to space.
Are we there yet?
I think we are because I can see the aliens in the dens.
There is a big alien and a bigger alien,
The bigger alien is bigger than the big alien.
'Hooo!' said the bigger alien,
'Eek!' said the big alien.
The bigger alien was magic,
It made the big alien small.
They showed me their den.
It was magical with bright, shiny, sparkling rocks
All colours of the rainbow.
They gave me a piece of cake and a drink of lemonade.
Then I said I'd have to go.
'Bye-bye' they said
And whoosh . . .
I was gone, back to my mum.

Hannah Spencer (7)
Redhill Primary School

MY FAVOURITE PLACE

S   pace is my favourite place
P   lanets orbit the sun
A   stronauts look at the Earth
C   omets whiz through the sky
E   verything is amazing!

Robert James Garner (9)
Redhill Primary School

A DREAM

I like to dream about dolphins,
Swimming and splashing free.

They jump up in the air,
And put water all over me.

Dolphins are so clever, they talk and sing
To each other.

And in my dream they say,
Happy birthday to each other.

I swim along with the dolphins,
They let me swim on their backs.

My dream ends suddenly when mum wakes me up,
It's time to get ready for school
No time to look back.

Rosie Hunter (7)
Redhill Primary School

SPACE

S   tars shine at night with their glittering light.
P   ictures are not as good as space in the human race.
A   ll the stars make a pattern as they lie in space.
C   an people go to the sun? It would burn and burn.
E   arth we live on as we rule.

Harry Stewart (9)
Redhill Primary School

A VOYAGE TO ROLLER WORLD

I leave Ockbrook at half-past two on a journey to Roller World.
It seems a long way, but I know it well,
As we travel by car along the A52 we go through the traffic lights,
Nearly all red they change quickly to green, on we go.
At the big island near the town, I think what a busy day!
But now I know we are nearly there, we are on Sir Frank Whittle Way.
I see the signs for Roller World, and some of my friends are here.
We put on our boots and whizz round the floor,
Coloured lights flashing and dazzling us more.
The music is loud as we dance and play games,
We have lots of laughs and a few bumps too,
Then it's our and we have to change.
We say our goodbyes and our thanks to the staff.
We tell them this visit will not be the last.
The journey home is very quick, green lights all the way.
I have had a super day
And it was free!

Grace Haspel (8)
Redhill Primary School

SPACE

S   hining, glittering stars.
P   eaceful, blue Pluto.
A   mazing, golden Saturn.
C   oming and going comets.
E   normous, blazing Jupiter.

Matthew Meadows (8)
Redhill Primary School

A Voyage In A Hot Air Balloon

We are going on a holiday in a hot air balloon,
I really hope we'll be there soon,
Up in the sky,
Floating so very high,
What is that I can see?
Yippee, it's the sea.
We must almost be there,
I am very excited because there's the fair,
Please can we go?
Mum says 'I think so,'
Hurrah!
This is going to be a fun holiday.

Connor Hewitson (7)
Redhill Primary School

Super Space

Misty moon,
　　Magical Mars,
Super space!
　　Jumbo Jupiter.
Powerful planets,
　　Super space!
Sparkling stars,
　　Naughty Neptune,
Super space!
　　Excellent Earth,
Sizzling sun,
　　Super space!

Becky Vesse (9)
Redhill Primary School

FRIENDS

Friends are kind
Friends are bossy
But I don't mind
Do you?

Friends are funny
Friends are nice
But we take jokes
Do you?

Friends are mates
Friends fall out
Friends are loving
Friends share.

Friends work with you
Friends care
Friends laugh
Friends come to your house.

Rosanna Langworthy (9)
Redhill Primary School

STARS

S   hiny glittering stars.
T   he gorgeous galaxy.
A   mazing Mars and naughty Neptune.
R   evolving Saturn.
S   uper space.

Ellis Potter (8)
Redhill Primary School

GUESS WHAT?

The animal looks like a furry rug
Like the biggest teddy bear in the world
Big sharp claws like dinosaurs' teeth
Roars like a jet engine.

Smells like muddy water
Like horrible, slushy water
Like germy fleas
Smells like dirty socks.

It likes to eat fish
All different kinds
Big, small, dead or alive fish
Scaly or silvery fish.

It feels like a furry rug
As comfy as a comfortable chair
As warm as a roaring hot fire
As soft as a panther.

Craig Seager (9)
Redhill Primary School

SPACE

S   mall, mouldy Pluto is so tiny.
P   lanets are round, some might be square.
A   year's gone by, the planets have stopped.
C   enturies have gone, the planets are spinning faster.
E   arth has stopped, we're all dead in bed.

Leigh Archer (8)
Redhill Primary School

A Voyage Of A Maths Test To India

I am in my cosy, extraordinary bed,
With many sums adding in my head.
Then I exploded out of my bed onto a rug,
When suddenly I felt a tug.

I saw numbers dashing all around,
Which did not make a sound.
On a board there were giant rules,
Of what to do and all about the magic tools.

I saw sums and thumped the numbers one by one,
At the end they were all correct and it was fun.
I got an extremely good prize,
A trip to India, what a surprise!

Susan Frankish (8)
Redhill Primary School

Space Is Wonderful

S   hooting stars race across the sky!
P   lanets float in space!
A   liens walk on their home planets!
C   rackling sun as the flames burn!
E   arth spins around.

Wonderful space!

Frankie Hollingworth (8)
Redhill Primary School

A Voyage Being Small In The Garden

I was playing one day in the sunny hot garden.
When I began to get smaller and smaller,
Until I was only bigger than a worm and smaller than a spider web.
Then something strange happened, an ant talked to me.
'Hello,' it said.
'Hello' I said back. 'Yuk, this mud is squashy.'
Then a spider talked to me,
'That's where Mr and Mrs Worm live,'
'Do they have children Mrs Spider?' I said.
'Don't know,' she said.
'Well anyway I'd better get back, it's my bedtime soon, so bye.' I said.
They all shouted bye back.

Jade McKenzie (7)
Redhill Primary School

Space

S   wivelling black hole spinning through with their partner worm hole.
P   lanets orbiting stars far and near, each planet depending
                                                  on their holy star.
A   liens eating each other from Mars, planning to attack
                                              each other every day.
C   entury from galaxy to galaxy but it takes
                                          five minutes through a worm hole.
E   arth eaters from Mars, planning to attack us when . . . *bang!*

Daniel Rowling (9)
Redhill Primary School

THE SHARK

I saw a shark.
I saw his teeth.
He got my leg
And pulled me beneath.
The water was cold.
I couldn't see.
I was so afraid.
Where could I be?
I escaped from his jaws.
I swam to the beach.
When I got there
I was out of reach.

Abby Mason (7)
Redhill Primary School

ANIMALS

Some crawling
Some falling.

Some eating
Some sleeping.

Some playing
Some laying.

Some flying
Some lying.

Some thumping
Some jumping.

Melissa Little (9)
Redhill Primary School

THE WILLOW

The willow sways
On wintry days.
The willow weeps
As it soundly sleeps.
The willow blows
And gently flows.
The willow cape
Keeps its shape.
The willow heaves
As it loses its leaves.
The willow is my favourite tree.

Victoria Richardson (9)
Redhill Primary School

SCHOOL DINNERS

Zombie's head,
Poisonous lead,
Werewolf hair,
Old smelly chair,
Leather purse,
Mummy's curse,
Witch's snot,
All in the pot,
Yummy, yum, yum.

Alex Smith (10)
Redhill Primary School

A VOYAGE TO THE SEASIDE

On my way to the seaside
I saw a boat,
It was a fishing boat,
We must be getting near.
When we get there
We are going to do some crabbing.

I can see the seaside.
Look there's lots of boats
There in the harbour.
Can we go crabbing now?
Yes, and then we have to go home.

James Elcock (8)
Redhill Primary School

A VOYAGE IN SPACE

Once there was a voyage in space.
A mission that was at stake in space.
There was going to be a meteorite,
The meteorite gave everyone a fright.
So eighty people went up to space to save the day.
They all had a bomb that was very powerful.
They were all happy leading to the meteorite.
With a plan to give it a good blast.
Right back into the past.
And they did.

Thomas Mills (7)
Redhill Primary School

IN THE FOREST

In the forest you will see,
Sun shining through a canopy.
Shadows of enormous trees,
And green leaves rustling in the breeze.

In the forest you will hear,
Buzzing of bees next to your ear.
A babbling stream that's running fast,
The song of the bird that's flying past.

In the forest you will smell,
The scent of flowers where they dwell.
The distinct aroma of evergreen trees
And faint odours carried by the breeze.

Anna Perkins (11)
Redhill Primary School

A VOYAGE IN THE SKY

I love to fly in an aeroplane
As it skims swiftly through the sky,
With clouds that look like candy floss
All white and fluffy and bright.
As I look out of my window
I see what's down below,
Cities, towns and villages that look like a patchwork quilt.
Oh how I love to fly in an aeroplane and watch the world go by.

Laura Barber (8)
Redhill Primary School

SPACE

Space
   Floating,
      Fast,
         Fiery,
            Freezing.

Space
   Never-ending,
      Empty,
         Quiet,
            Gloomy.

Space
   Glorious,
      Wonderful,
         Golden,
            Starry.

Space,
   Shining.

Space, space, space.

Elliot Emery (9)
Redhill Primary School

A VOYAGE TO A HIDDEN ISLAND

A hidden island far away
Where hidden people laugh and play
We set sail to find you there,
A secret voyage, a trick, a dare.
We long to seek, we have to know
The island hidden long ago.

Emma Little (7)
Redhill Primary School

A VOYAGE UNDER WATER, BUT

One day I went under the sea,
When we got deep it was nice and warm under the sea but,
When we were under the sea,
There was a treasure on the sand,
But . . .
There's a shark!
A big bubble came out of its mouth but
It didn't scare me.
I picked up the treasure and got into the bubble but,
The treasure tipped up and out fell the gold,
Back down to the sand but,
I'll come back for it when I get old.

James Lapping (8)
Redhill Primary School

A VOYAGE ACROSS AFRICA

This is a story about my family and me
And how we travelled to Africa to see what we could see.
We started in the desert and all we saw was sand,
We walked and walked for miles and miles till we could hardly stand.
Then we came to the jungle, the animals were squawking and
chattering,
Then we saw a lion, he was fierce and growling at us.
When it was time to go home we all felt quite sad,
But then we saw our pets back home we all felt quite glad.

Abigail Teflise (8)
Redhill Primary School

A Voyage Out Of A City

I scrambled through a dark and creepy wood
With golden leaves on the ground
Giving way to golden sand.
I saw the sea
It was bashing and crashing.
A submarine waited for me to go
Under the raging sea.

James McKinnon (8)
Redhill Primary School

A Voyage In Space

This wide open space is a strange sort of place,
Where man goes by rocket to the moon
To watch the sun light up the planets,
Such as Earth, Saturn and Mars,
But best of all those bright shiny stars.
What an amazing place this wide open space is.

Luke Spinks (7)
Redhill Primary School

Space

Stars shine at night.
Stars are really bright.
Planets are nice.
Planets are so nice.
Planets are blue and yellow.
Space is cool.

Josh Woods (8)
Redhill Primary School

GLITTERING STARS

Shiny stars glitter in the dark sky.
Polished moon glitters in the glittering sky.
Aqua Neptune lightens up in the dark sky.
Earth, the cold seas and grassy lands.
I love space.

Amy Davies (8)
Redhill Primary School

AMAZING SPACE

Planets turning in . . . space!
Shiny moon floating in . . . space!
Silver stars sparkling in . . . space!
Golden sun hanging in . . . space!
Black and infinite
That is *amazing space!*

Hattie Owens (8)
Redhill Primary School

WHY IS SPACE . . .

I don't know why
Space is in the sky.
I thought that space was on the ground,
But why,
But why
Space is in the sky?

Jessica Smyth (8)
Redhill Primary School

THE VOLCANO

White hot trees of fire,
Heading skyward higher and higher.

Lava engulfing everything in its path,
Plants burnt by its fiery warmth.

Inside from where nothing or no one has returned,
Where rocks and magma together are churned.

Rocks catapulted into the air,
Blistering lava descends without a care.

Robert Howarth (10)
Redhill Primary School

A VOYAGE DOWN TO TITANIC

We are ready to dive captain,
Okay Smith.
Ready, steady, go!
Full power to thrust
And take her down,
Low, low, low.
We'll find Titanic in her resting place
In the dark and gloomy sea
And this is where she will stay for all eternity.

Benjamin Harrison (8)
Redhill Primary School

FOREST

In this forest no humans walk.
Owls hoot softly, breaking the night silence.

Eerie blackness protecting the forest.
The old woodcutter's hut showing no signs of life.

Old trees creaking in the reckless wind.
A stream nearby giving animals fresh water.

Kestrels looking for prey in vain.
In this forest no humans walk.

Jonathan Meadows (11)
Redhill Primary School

BIRTHDAY

B   eautiful baby born today
I   n our mother's arms you gently lay
R   ound the bedroom we all stand
T   oday's the day we all waited for
H   ooray she's born!
D   arling baby, more precious than fairy dust
A   ll safe and sound and snug as a bug
Y   our birthday has arrived at last.

Harriet Cronin (8)
Redhill Primary School

WHERE THE WATERFALL IS

Where the waterfall is
I can hear
The gentle flapping of the bird,
Bees buzzing in a rose,
The nearby bushes rustling and
The silence of the water running by.

Where the waterfall is
I can see the shadows of the creatures passing by,
The babbling of the crystal clear water,
The sun cracking through the clouds and
Water like a constantly running tap.

Where the waterfall is
I can feel
The cool spray from the waterfall,
The cold breeze and
The splashes of the water falling into the plunge pool
As if it is in a diving competition.

Where the waterfall is
I can smell
The sweet scent of the flowers and
The smell of the pine needles from the mountain forest.

Lucy Laing (11)
Redhill Primary School

WATERFALL

Wet, wet waterfall,
Gushing, gleaming, clear,
Rushing down jagged cliffs,
Like a salted tear.

Wet, wet waterfall,
Spray as cold as ice,
Droplets from the top,
Like waving white kites.

Michael Pearson (11)
Redhill Primary School

MY VERY OWN FOREST

In my very own forest I hear
The call of birds,
The trickle of a stream and
The rustle of leaves.

In my very own forest I smell
Rotting bark,
Oak trees and
The scent of flowers.

In my very own forest I feel
The spray of the stream,
The falling of the leaves and
The feet of birds on my shoulder.

In my very own forest I see
Winding branches,
Beautiful flowers and a
Sparkling stream.

Richard Webster-Noble (10)
Redhill Primary School

THE JUNGLE

In the jungle tall trees tower all around,
The sun shines off their green leaves,
Noisy monkeys howl as they leap from tree to tree,
Making loud noises as they hang onto branches.

A river flows through the trees splashing on its banks,
With crocodiles resting on its banks,
Prowling leopards stalk their prey,
As they patrol past trees.

Sloths cling to the tree trunks slowly climbing,
As they eat leaves and watch life below,
While scaly snakes slide along the ground,
Colourful birds fly around and sit in trees.

Luke McKinnon (10)
Redhill Primary School

MOUNTAINS

M iserable people whining to go back home but can't.
O verhung rocks as jagged as twenty bushes of thorns.
U ntouched caverns cursed and full of danger.
N umb fingers of suffering people in the blistering cold.
T ragic injuries which could cause death.
A blizzard hits like the toughest person throwing steel at people.
I nteresting fossils being found in the snow by survivors.
N itro blasts, causing great avalanches.
S weating people jumping in happiness for returning to their families.

Richard Hannaford (10)
Redhill Primary School

FOREST

The trees swaying from side to side,
From the hard blowing wind.
The sound of owls hooting high above the trees
And the noise which is like
Lots of different animals trying to sing.
High above on the trees,
Leaves falling off.

Michael Evans (11)
Redhill Primary School

SPACE

S   hiny stars glitter in the darkness.
P   olished moon so mystical and cold.
A   qua Neptune so polished in the dark.
C   apital sun, so hot, searing.
E   arth is where we live, it's nice here.

Fay Garratt (8)
Redhill Primary School

SPACE

S   un is the hottest place in space.
P   lace I like best is angry, red Mars.
A   planet is orange Saturn.
C   ector 946 Earth.
E   normous Jupiter.

Jonathan Levers (9)
Redhill Primary School

FOOTBALL MATCH

People waiting
People singing
People yelling
Players come out
Referee blows
The players attack.

Managers shouting
Defenders tackling
A player shoots
The goalie misses
The stadium erupts.

Corners, throw-ins, free kicks.
Yellow card, red card, fancy tricks.
At 90 minutes the game ends,
The crowd cheers
Scarves wave.

Mark Banks (10)
Redhill Primary School

WATERFALL

A waterfall foaming white like snow.
The crashing water thundering on the rocks below.
Rushing over the edge like an April shower,
The spray just steams with magic power.
Fast flowing like a hare speeding by,
The water splashes over small pebbles and ripples try.
And they break into soft mossy rocks and babble along.
It bubbles and gurgles like a happy song.

Charlotte Little (11)
Redhill Primary School

THE MOUNTAIN

T   he great, great mountain
H   uge giant waterfalls
E   ngulfing mounds of scree.

M   iles of land before it
O   ut in front a garden of hummocks
U   nusual wildlife seen only on mountains
N   o way to some parts
T   errain as rough as a hedgehog's back
A   t the anchor magma hot
I   n the sky eagles fly
N   ot a soul in sight.

Oliver Cooper (11)
Redhill Primary School

THE ARAB

As she canters swiftly with the wind
The sun shining on her chestnut coat
She feeds in the greenest fields
And roams on the softest grass
With grace and beauty she looks around
When her playmate comes in to sight
She trots up to the grey Camargue
And they gallop off up the field.

Eleanor O'Connor (10)
Richardson Endowed Primary School

My Grandpa Is Amazing

My grandpa is amazing
He draws brilliant trains
He even plays golf
At his old age.

We go on magical journeys
Across oceans and seas
We go to the land of Oz
There's a forest of trees.

I love my grandpa
He's always right
He even climbs pylons
To fetch down my kite.

That was the story of my grandpa
You can tell he's not lazy
He really is very great
My grandpa is amazing.

Laura Drury (9)
Richardson Endowed Primary School

My Teacher

My teacher's nice
My teacher's kind
My teacher's rude
And sometimes in a mood.

My teacher's clever
My teacher's smart
She's very good at maths
And really good at art.

My teacher sometimes shouts
And I sometimes get cross
I know she doesn't mean it
Because she's the boss.

Kimberley Williamson (10)
Richardson Endowed Primary School

THE CHALLENGE

My name's on the programme
I'm starting to get the flow
Bang! Bang! Bang! Goes the gun
One more race to go.

It's me, it's my turn
Hearts beating fast
Standing on the starting block
How long can this last?

We are taking our marks
Bang goes the gun . . .
I dive in, splash!
I'm now on the run.

Can I win the race?
The roar of the crowd
My mum's smiling face
My dad standing proud.

My name's over the tannoy
I collect my prize
A warm, warm feeling
The race is mine.

Sarah Herbert (10)
Richardson Endowed Primary School

THE MOONLIGHT

Moonlight, the only light.
Moonlight, the busiest light.
Moonlight the only moon to bring the light.
The beady-eyed cat goes wandering in the dim moonlight.
The owls go hooting twit-twoo in the moonlight.
The moonlight brings our light, the only light.
Moonlight is the only light.
Moonlight is the brightest light.
Moonlight, moonlight, moonlight.

The fox is hunting for its prey in the moonlight.
The hedge hogs hiding from its predator
Sticking out its spikes in the moonlight.
Badgers gobbling up worms, slugs and fruit,
In the rising moonlight.
Moonlight is the only light.
Moonlight is the brightest light.
Moonlight, moonlight, moonlight.

Laura Mason (10)
Richardson Endowed Primary School

A SCHOOL FOOL

When I first went to school.
I thought it was a swimming pool,
And I thought classrooms,
Were glass-rooms,
I thought pencils
Were Strepsils,
I lied,
I kept it all inside.

Matthew Measures (10)
Richardson Endowed Primary School

I DON'T BELIEVE A BIT

My dad's an alligator
But gets warmed up on a radiator
He always needs to eat a pea
But has to do it in the sea.
Then one day he got forced by a shark
To go and live on Noah's ark.
When one day he got off the ark
He saw a dog that went 'Bark, bark, bark.'
He had to go and live in a kennel
Which was right beside the English Channel.

James O'Brien (9)
Richardson Endowed Primary School

SAM AND ROSIE

My dog Sam is as gentle as a lamb.
My dog Rosie's life is very, very cosy.

They jump and play both day and night,
Their life is full of pleasure and delight.

They make me happy, they make me sad,
They're mostly good but sometimes bad.

They're black as night, with eyes so bright.
To own them is a pure delight.

Abby Noble (9)
Ripley Junior School

OUR HOUSE

It's really weird at our house,
Mum's a walking book
Dad's as quiet as a mouse
Brother's a crazy cook.
Sinks that talk,
Automatic doors,
No peace and quiet,
Squeaky floors,
Bedtime, that's the worst
When my dad snores
It sounds like he's burst.
Getting dressed, my sister's mad,
She dresses up just like my dad.
After that it's time for school
A boy called David
He's a right big fool,
Plays with a boy called David
And man that boy is stupid.

Rhys Evans (9)
Ripley Junior School

THE DAISY

In a coloured meadow
Near a lonely tree,
Stands a little daisy,
No bigger than a bee.

In a coloured meadow,
Dancing by a tree,
Floats a little daisy
Smaller than the smallest tree.

In a coloured meadow,
Who knows what can be found,
Look at the little daisy
Sitting on the ground.

Rachel Bailey (10)
Ripley Junior School

THE SECRET GARDEN

Behind the door,
Lies the gate,
To my secret garden.

I opened the gate,
And I looked inside,
What I saw was beautiful.

I slowly tiptoed,
Down the steps,
Then as I walked I was amazed.

I looked around me,
Blooming flowers surrounded me,
I sat upon a flowered bench.

I looked up and saw a butterfly,
It was pretty, it was small,
The little butterfly shook my hand.

Then in the morning breeze,
My little butterfly flew away,
She flew so high

As I said 'Goodbye.'

Aimee Ratcliffe (10)
Ripley Junior School

CATS

Big cats in the jungle,
Small cats in the house,
Big cats find their own food,
Small cats catch a mouse,
Some with spots and some with stripes,
Whiskers twitching in the night,
Eyes that glow in the dark,
Creeping silently in the park,
A roar, a growl, a snarl or a snap
Always aware of a deadly man trap,
Cars go racing down the street,
Cats' eyes light up as they meet,
Lions in the safety of their pride,
Cats all snug, cosy and warm inside,
Big teeth chew on raw meat
Small tongues lap their milk so sweet
Lying softly in the sun
These days really are such fun.

Cassie Dye (10)
Ripley Junior School

FROST PICTURES

In winter, jumping from my bed
To part my curtains, blue and red
I see upon the window pane
A frosty fairy land again;

As though a secret, magic hand
Had painted there a wonderland
Of frozen ferns and castles tall
And sparkling flowers large and small.

But when the sun begins to rise,
With tears so dazzling to my eyes
The magic pictures quickly pass
And leave just water on the glass.

Natalie Pickering (10)
Ripley Junior School

JUNK YARD

My bedroom's full of sweet wrappers
And bubblegum that's solid
I think it looks how bedrooms should
My mum says it looks horrid.

So I tidied up my bedroom
'Cause my mum told me so
My smelly socks went in the wash
I knew they had to go.

The bubblegum went in the bin
I recycled the sweet wrappers
And from the feast I had last week
I chucked the mouldy crackers.

My bedroom's very tidy now
My mum is over the moon
But I know one thing for sure
It won't be tidy soon.

Sally Archer (11)
Ripley Junior School

A SEASIDE TALE

Buckets and spades
Also arcades,
Ships and boats
No need for coats.
Lots of sand
And little hands,
Walk down the pier
To see the fish swim near,
When the tide comes in
There's no time for a swim.
There's fun and games for everyone,
Until Saturday comes,
And the car engine hums.

Katie Dale (9)
Ripley Junior School

CATS

Cats chase rats
But they don't like bats.
Some cats are fat
Some cats are flat.
They bring you presents
Like dead pheasants.
Cats can come in all sizes
Sometimes you might win prizes.
But anyhow
My cat just goes meow.

Rachel McKenzie (8)
Ripley Junior School

WILLY THE WORM

At the ground I begin to dig,
I hit my head on a large twig
As I enter the slushy mud,
I see a dead flower bud,
As along my dark trail,
I come across a slimy snail.
When I see a big bug,
A beetle behind me gives me a tug,
It says to me 'What a nice day
But be careful if you're going *that* way.'

Well now it's time to say goodbye,
But then again, ouch, a bird got me in the eye.

Sam Turner (10)
Ripley Junior School

BUBBLES

It's so lovely blowing bubbles;
To watch them grow is fun.
They are so full of beautiful rainbow patterns
That shimmer in the sun.

I wish that I was a pretty bubble
And float up to the blue sky,
To see the house way down below
While I'm flying high.

But bubbles burst of course!
Those shinny small balls.
And when you catch them in your hand
There's nothing left at all.

Louise Smith (8)
Ripley Junior School

I WANNABE A WALLABY

I wannabe a wallaby,
  A wallaby, that's true,
    Don't wannabe a possum,
      A koala or a 'roo.
        I wanna go a-hopping,
          Anywhere I please,
            Hopping without stopping,
              Through eucalyptus trees.
                A wallaby, a wallaby,
                  That's what I wannabe,
                    I'd swap myself to be one,
                      But a problem I can see.
                    If I can find a wallaby,
                      A very friendly wallaby,
                        Who would really, really, really . . .
                      Wannabe me!

Ami Rawson (9)
Ripley Junior School

THE WORM

The worm is very, very long
It moves around.
It moves carefully on the ground,
But it does not make a sound.
When it moves it says 'Hush, hush'
But the worm is never in a rush.
It turns left, right, centre and around,
Five minutes later it's gone!
It's gone under the ground.

Natasha Brough (9)
Ripley Junior School

THE MYSTERY ANIMAL

Tongue–licker
Tail-wagger
Meat-eater
Cat-catcher
Nose-sniffer
Teeth-ripper
Water-drinker
Fast-runner
Loud-barker.

Lexy Else (11)
Ripley Junior School

RABBITS

Rabbits, rabbits, rabbits,
That's all they talk about.
Rabbits
They talk about rabbits at school
And everywhere I go
Everyone talks about rabbits.
Do you know what my favourite thing is?
Rabbits.

Charlotte Day (8)
Ripley Junior School

THE CHANGING SEASONS

Spring, summer, autumn, winter, every year the same.
Round and round the seasons go like a party game.

Spring is before summer, blossom on the trees.
Flying around up in the air there are buzzing bees.

Spring, summer, autumn, winter, every year the same.
Round and round the seasons go like a party game.

Summer is before autumn, there are lots of different trees,
Hanging from their branches are multicoloured leaves.

Spring, summer, autumn, winter, every year the same.
Round and round the seasons go like a party game.

Autumn is before winter, the leaves begin to fall.
Children are playing outside with a bat and ball.

Spring, summer, autumn, winter, every year the same.
Round and round the seasons go like a party game.

Winter is the last to come, this is the happiest time you know.
Santa is on his way again, the gardens are full of snow.

Spring, summer, autumn, winter, every year the same.
Round and round the seasons go like a party game.

Carly Howard (10)
St Werburgh's Primary School, Spondon

THE AUTUMN THIEF

Whistling through came the autumn wind
Stealing the trees' brown bark.
Whoosh! Straight through the leaves,
Went the autumn wind.
Everything in the woods looking very sad.
The autumn wind not feeling bad.

All the trees very cold,
But the autumn thief does not care,
For it is he who has no heart.
You see he does not care
Because he will be back again
To take what you see there.

Andrew Marriott (11)
St Werburgh's Primary School, Spondon

HARRY POTTER

Harry Potter of Hogwart's School,
He's so good, he's really cool,
He's got a friend, Hermione ('Her-may-o-nee')
She's as nice as nice can be.

The Weasleys are Ron, Ginny, George and Fred
And Percy the eldest, who's a real big-head.
Harry's enemy Draco Malfoy,
Is a really horrible boy!

Harry's cousin Dudley is spoilt rotten,
But Harry is always forgotten.
Harry's owl is called Hedwig,
As owls go he's very big.

Hagrid is a giant man,
He teaches 'creatures' when he can,
And then there's Professor Snape,
Be careful he could change your shape.

And then there is one more yet,
Who we really can't forget,
He who should not be named – Voldemort
Who will kill Harry if he's caught.

Abigail Knapp (9)
St Werburgh's Primary School, Spondon

THE GARDEN

When you first go in the garden,
You know its everlasting bliss.
Flowers and trees are all around
And there's a pond with silver fish.

There are sunlit fruit trees in a row,
Bearing lots of delicious fruit.
Ruby apples, scarlet cherries
And sweet pears in a golden suit.

The flowers, oh what a joy to see!
Dressed in colourful rainbow petals.
Bees busily around the poppies,
The daisies and the stinging nettles.

There's a rockery in one corner
With a waterfall sparkling bright.
Fish play in the pond at the bottom,
Scales glistening in the light.

Round the garden there's a holly hedge,
With red berries to look its best.
The glossy bush has small hollows,
Safe corners for sparrows to nest.

In the middle there's a lawn
With lush grass, sweet and green.
At one side there's some vegetables,
The finest anyone has seen.

When you first go in the garden,
You know its everlasting bliss.
Flowers and trees are all around
And there's a pond with silver fish.

Jessica Langton (10)
St Werburgh's Primary School, Spondon

THE CANAL

I'm flowing through the fields green,
I see everything you've seen.
I trickle and I splash,
But I never, ever crash.
Because I am the canal,
And I go on forever.

I see the bikers, riding past,
I see the joggers, jogging fast.
I see the walkers, walking tall,
I see the animals, dark and small.
Because I am the canal,
And I go on forever.

I flow through the meadows until I stop,
I halt right outside the lock.
I wait so long and then the barge,
Opens the gate, and lets me charge.
Because I am the canal,
And I go on forever.

I flow through night and day,
My feet start to ache, so I say:
'Let me free, let me free,
Come rescue me.'
Because I am the canal,
And I have to stay here
Forever!

Sarah Broomfield (10)
St Werburgh's Primary School, Spondon

MY NAUGHTY LITTLE SISTER

My little sister is very naughty
Sometimes though she's very sporty
She has a friend who's called Bad Harry
And his best friend is Naughty Gary.
Sometimes they go over the top
And then we have to make them stop.

One bright, breezy, sunny day.
When we were out in the bay,
She was splashing in the water
The tide, it nearly came and caught her!
Like a fish in a fisherman's net.
When she got out she was very wet.

One day she got a teacher's note
And to my mum it was wrote.
How my sister had been bad
It made my sister very sad
And ever since she got that letter,
My little sister has been better.

So my sister has learnt her lesson!

Emily Langton (8)
St Werburgh's Primary School, Spondon

ENORMOUS ELEPHANT

Get out of the way,
I'm marching through the jungle,
I'm the first in line of the marching band,
My trunk is my trumpet.

I love to have a bath,
With the other musicians,
I like to eat bananas,
And I like to eat a lot of other fruit.

Charlotte Rodgers (11)
St Werburgh's Primary School, Spondon

MY PONY FLOSSY

My pony Flossy is completely grey,
As she canters round the field every day,
She's got a golden bridle which goes round her nose,
She thinks she's a champion and likes to pose,
She's got a long silver mane and tail,
And her mate is Abigail.

She likes to eat hay and wheat,
She likes me to give her a treat,
She's strong and tough,
You wouldn't like to play with her,
She's too rough.
Her ears prick up,
In a horse show at Castle of Horses,
When she's got the cup.

She can't get on the train,
So she gallops along the lane,
When it lets off steam she gallops again.
I teach her everything,
Including chomp, chomp, chomp.

Nicol Winfield (8)
St Werburgh's Primary School, Spondon

THE CLOCK

It's 7 o'clock, time to arise
Down the stairs before you open your eyes.
A quick wash and brush, then into the car
Off to school, it isn't that far.

Up to the school gates, made it on time,
One minute later, a punishable crime.
It seems that the clock is running your life.
You're constantly staring, it gives you such strife.

Straight into school work, no time for a break.
By ten they say 'Four lessons to take.'
It's time for a snack, a rest for a while.
In comes the teacher, with Cheshire cat smile.

He's caught me talking to my friend by my side,
He says 'If you keep talking, your school work will slide.'
So it's back to the grindstone, this isn't so cool,
I whisper under my breath 'Silly old fool.'

Jessica Gallagher (9)
St Werburgh's Primary School, Spondon

THE SEA AND THE SHORE

Said the shore to the sea,
'I do not want to make friends with thee,
because you make me wet and a mess,
and you call me Jess when my name is Bess.'

'I want to be friends for evermore,'
said the sea to the shore,
'because I love the way we play,
all the live, long day!'

'I know you do and I kind of like to
so . . . I think I will be friends with you!'
So the sea and the shore,
Were best friends for evermore.

Emma Shore (10)
St Werburgh's Primary School, Spondon

I WANT A RABBIT!

'I want a rabbit!'
'No you don't!'
'Yes I do!'

I have a little rabbit and her name is Flopsy May
She nibbles all the time and when I bring her inside
She even nibbles what's mine.
'I still want a rabbit!'
'No you don't!'
I have a little rabbit and her name is Flopsy May
I take her for a walk every night and day.
'I still want a rabbit!'
'No you don't!'
I have a little rabbit and her name is Flopsy May
Although she's as soft as a bear,
She's as naughty as a hare.

I don't want a rabbit!

Alice Williamson (10)
St Werburgh's Primary School, Spondon

ALIENS

And . . . and what are they like?
Oh they are both equally mean,
They are both ugly and green
One fat and the other lean
Their names are Boggis and Bean.

Today I saw them again
They stared at me as I worried
With my McDonald's McFlurry
I hurried home to my mummy,
On my way I dropped my McFlurry
When I got home I saw my mummy
She was making me a curry.

Now I don't go to see
Big Boggis and leaning Bean
Cos they gang up on me
Like one heck of a team.

Daniel Metcalf (9)
St Werburgh's Primary School, Spondon

THERE'S A LITTLE ANGEL

There's a little angel,
Sitting in the trees,
Up in the sky,
Are the clouds and bees.

Laugh at me,
And I laugh at you,
For there's an angel,
Shouting boo.

I'm a little angel,
In a cool breeze,
Looking around at,
The birds in the trees.

I'm a little angel,
Saying goodbye,
And the wings on my back,
Shall begin to rise.

Sean Shields (10)
St Werburgh's Primary School, Spondon

SEASIDE FUN

When I go to the seaside,
I like to dig in the sand.
I like to look for pretty shells
And hold them in my hand.
I like to have an ice cream to make me really cool
Then I go and jump in the big blue pool.

I sometimes like to go looking,
For little crabs and fish,
And if I'm lucky and find some,
I put them in a dish.
I like to dig sandcastles and make a little moat,
Then I go and get my big, blue boat,
And watch it sail and float.
But all too soon it's time to go home because the day is done,
And I think about tomorrow when I'll have some more fun.

Josie Hardaker (9)
St Werburgh's Primary School, Spondon

THE ALIEN

He had a green face
And blue hair
He's big and fat
Like a grizzly bear.
But he learnt to care.

He was a fright
And a terrible sight
Especially at night
When it wasn't light.

He loved to eat fruit
And lots of meat
Especially children's feet.

And when they got up
He would eat their seat.
When they played games
He would always cheat.

Bradley Larimore (9)
St Werburgh's Primary School, Spondon

THE MYSTERY

'Hello,' echoed the voice of the girl,
In the old dusty room;
And her brother waiting, standing,
On the jewelled grass, under the moon.

And the tiny pinprick stars,
On the dark blue sky,
And the whistling, blowing wind,
Brushing against the trees, a cry.

Becky Cussens (11)
St Werburgh's Primary School, Spondon

FELINE

I love you, I love you, I really do,
Give me some food and I'll stay with you.
Fussing and purring on her knee,
Waiting for my tasty tea.
Make her happy when she's sad,
Never smacks me when I'm bad.
Bring a bird to the door,
Gives me a rub on my jaw,
Now it's time to say goodbye,
Because I made my real owners cry.
I love you, I love you, I really do,
And I'll never forget the good times with you.

Cher Maxwell (10)
St Werburgh's Primary School, Spondon

WHY . . .?

Why do people go to the moon?
Does a flute have a tune?
How far does the sea reach?
Would you like a peach?
Where does the blue sky end?
Is it straight or does it have a bend?
Why do we have white clouds in the sky?
Is there a fly nearby?
Do you like bread?
Or have you a big head?
Do you like light or dark?
Or does your dog bark?

Christina Ford (10)
St Werburgh's Primary School, Spondon

IN A SPACE ROCKET

In a space rocket floating afar,
In and out, in and out, like a gliding star.

Floating in a space rocket far and far,
They've made the rocket out of metal and tar.

Ashes to ashes, dust to dust,
The metal rocket is starting to rust.

In a metal rocket floating away,
Come back another day.

Hitting the atmosphere, alert, alert,
Out of control, blurt, blurt!

The metal rocket is landing safely.

Paris Sullivan (9)
St Werburgh's Primary School, Spondon

THE ALIEN

And . . . and what is he like?
Oh he's wormy and squirmy,
He's scary and hairy,
He's gloomy and roomy,
And that's what he's like.

And . . . and what does he eat?
Oh he eats his beans and his greens,
He eats worms and germs,
He eats meat and feet,
And that's what he eats.

And . . . and where does he live?
Oh he lives in a mouse and a house,
He lives with me instead of in a tree,
He lives in a pen instead of a den,
And that's where he lives.

Shannon Smith (8)
St Werburgh's Primary School, Spondon

WHINNY WITCH

And . . . and what is Whinny Witch like?
She has got a spot on her nose
And one on her toes.

She's called Keylie,
She is a nice witch,
She does magic,
And lots of tricks.
She eats people for her tea,
She also eats porridge,
When she visits me,
So she's not very horrid.

She wears a pointy hat,
With a same coloured dress
And a bow on her cape
And she looks like a mess.

Keylie Banyard (9)
St Werburgh's Primary School, Spondon

WAITING FOR TOMORROW

As I looked out of my window last night
I saw an endless pattern of rooftops,
In each window, a light.

Cars in the drives and curtains were drawn.
I was suddenly tired and began to yawn.
I got into bed thoughts filling my head.
And as I lay there quietly thinking,
I seemed to see somebody winking.

It's God I thought, then he began to say,
'Tomorrow will be a wonderful day.
The sun will shine brightly with a golden gleam,
The most beautiful day you've ever seen.'

And so I drifted off to sleep,
I dreamed of the morning and the promise it would keep.

Dominic Hill (9)
St Werburgh's Primary School, Spondon

THE GARBAGE MAN

And . . . and what is he like?
Oh he's green and mean and a little tyke.
He's bubbly and fat and he's metal,
He's a man who does not have a bike,
He's mad and a good lad and a nettle.

And . . . and what does he eat?
He eats loaves of bread and meat,
Oh he eats toenails and people,
And soup and bread and beans and feet.

And . . . and where does he live?
Oh he lives in the garbage,
With bananas and goo,
He loves a human being in a stew.

Louis Danvers (8)
St Werburgh's Primary School, Spondon

ANIMALS

We have animals in our homes,
These are known as pets,
Dogs, cats, rabbits, birds,
Most animals don't like vets.

We take our pets walking
Some run after thrown sticks,
Whilst cats go out alone
Dogs have to learn tricks.

Pets come in sizes
Either small or big,
Some have beautiful colours
From a mouse to a great big pig.

Animals are there once you get to know them.

Natasha Waring (8)
St Werburgh's Primary School, Spondon

ANIMALS

I'd like to meet an elephant,
With a big, long trunk,
He could live in my back garden,
Amongst all my junk.

I'd like to meet a dolphin,
Swimming in the sea,
He could be my best friend
And would always play with me.

I'd like to meet a rattle snake,
Slithering through the grass,
He'd be multicoloured,
I could show him to the class.

I'd like to meet an octopus,
And shake him by the hand,
I'd remember his happy face,
When he joined my old school band.

I'd like to meet a crocodile,
With his knobbly green skin,
I could ask him if he'd like my lunch,
As he's looking rather thin.

I'd like to meet a polar bear,
With his soft, white fur,
I told my cat I'd seen him,
But all she said was purr.

Amy Milwain (8)
St Werburgh's Primary School, Spondon

THE CROCODILE

And . . . and what is he like?
Oh, he's ugly and gloomy,
He's green and bubbly,
He's spooky and gooey.

And . . . and what does he eat?
Oh, he eats people and feet,
And grass and meat,
He eats fish and stew,
And boys and goo.

And . . . and where does he live?
Oh, he lives in a swamp,
Just like a flomp.

Grant James Ellis (8)
St Werburgh's Primary School, Spondon

GRAN!

My gran's so annoying
She eats these funny pears
She chews sticky toffee
Sometimes even chairs.

She stares like a zombie
And snores when she sleeps
And calls me baby Lucy
And gives me loads of sweets.

Guess what? She's not so bad.
But the thing I like most,
My gran's never sad!

Lucy D'Amico (8)
St Werburgh's Primary School, Spondon

THE TEACHER

And . . . and what is he like?
Oh he's big and mean,
He's horrible and lean,
He's clever and tall,
He's stupid and tall.

And . . . and what does he eat?
Oh feet and a treat,
And trees and bees.

And . . . and where does he live?
Oh he lives in his glasses
And it smashes and crashes.
All day long his breath pongs,
He lines up in a line,
He cannot tell the time.

Jordan Trewhella (8)
St Werburgh's Primary School, Spondon

LITTLE BALLERINA

I am a ballerina, I am such a pretty thing,
And when I'm spinning round and round I love to laugh and sing.
I sometimes like to imagine I'm a star in a show,
And I can hear the people clapping, I feel all aglow.
I do my little spins and turns and a beautiful pirouette,
I wish I could ballet round the world, but I'm not big enough yet.
But one day when I'm older and I've got a new tutu,
I hope that all my dreams will come true.

Georgia Hardaker (8)
St Werburgh's Primary School, Spondon

THE GRINCH

And . . . and what is he like?
He's green and mean,
And he likes riding a bike.
He's a funny shape
And not often seen.

And . . . and what does he eat?
He likes to eat meat and feet
And he likes to dance to a beat.

And . . . and where does he live?
He lives under my bed
And likes to be fed.

Lucy Siena (8)
St Werburgh's Primary School, Spondon

MY PET WAS MADE

I built my pet
She's not ready quite yet
I made her out of sticks
It's better than bricks
I gave her a pattern
Made of ticks
I thought I'd teach her lots of tricks.

Charli Lawson (8)
St Werburgh's Primary School, Spondon

THE ALIEN

Oh he's squishy and slimy,
He's gungy and spongy.

He's blue and green,
And never seen.

He sometimes eats a bug,
And he sits on a rug.

When he's in a race
He needs lots of space.

When he's mad he goes purple,
And smashes the shell of a turtle.

You should see his face,
When he's packing his holiday case.

Jodie Allen (9)
St Werburgh's Primary School, Spondon

MY PET RABBIT

Oh she's white and bright,
She likes to fly my kite,
She flies in the light,
And has a bad bite.

When I pull her ears,
Down comes a lot of tears,
When I opened the door,
My rabbit was eating straw.

She runs round the house,
All through the night,
When I open the door,
She gives me a fright.

Shona Mackenzie (9)
St Werburgh's Primary School, Spondon

GOLDY MY DOG

She's cuddly and furry,
Happy and fluffy,
Loving and buffy,
Sometimes stuffy.

She eats spiders and meat,
She nibbles your feet,
She woofs and barks,
When she's at the park.

She knocks things over,
She's quiet in a Rover,
When she looks into your eyes,
It makes you want to cry.

That's my Goldy!

Emma Poxon (8)
St Werburgh's Primary School, Spondon

THE MOON

The moon is a ball,
And she flies in her misty veil,
She eats horrible snails.

And feels the clouds
She is so pale
She appears to be a quail.

She has bright eyes
And counts ploughs
And likes cows.

Abigail Wright (8)
St Werburgh's Primary School, Spondon

WINTER CHILL

W e shiver in our shoes.
I   cicles hanging from the roofs.
N umb feet in the cold.
T   ingling fingers in the bitter.
E   verything is always white.
R   ivers lost under Earth.

C   hilly breeze on our faces.
H   ills slippery and slidey.
I   shiver as I go home.
L   ittle children making snowmen.
L   ittle children getting warm.

Cara Kowalczuk (9)
Shelton Junior School

WILD WINTER

W inter days are waiting.
I cy concrete beneath our feet.
L ots of freezing children in the cold playground.
D ays of winter are so long.

W e shiver in our shoes.
I n the school is very warm.
N umb fingers are very, very cold.
T oes are wildly tingling.
E verybody is wearing a hat.
R oads are very slippery.

James Glasby (8)
Shelton Junior School

FROSTY DAY

F reezing in the morning,
R ather cold at night,
O h it's very cold, I get frostbite,
S o I was in pain all night through,
T oday I'll go to the doctor because I've got flu.
Y our frostbite does hurt too.

D ad let me sleep for
A rather long time
Y esterday was new year and I got rid of my flu.

Tyler Oliver (9)
Shelton Junior School

I'M AN AMBULANCE

I'm an ambulance, a very fast ambulance
On the look out foe people being hurt
I make people live so they will get better
If people are hurt the police send a letter.

I'm an ambulance, a very fast ambulance
On the look out for people that are poorly,
I can go fast, I can go slow,
When people try and trick me I say no.

I'm an ambulance, a very fast ambulance
On the look out for people being hurt
I listen to my din with my white and black skin
I am hard and solid I'm made out of tin.

I'm an ambulance a very fast ambulance,
On the look out for people that are poorly
I make a loud noise
A banging noise.

Adam Yates (8)
Shelton Junior School

ADJECTIVES FOR BREAKFAST

Juicy, fattening, sizzling, beautiful bacon,
Sizzling, beautiful, juicy, fattening bacon,
Beautiful, sizzling, bacon, juicy, fattening,
Bacony, juicy, fattening, beautiful, sizzle,
Fattening, beautiful, juicy, sizzling bacon,
Juicy, fattening, sizzling, bacony, beautiful,
Sizzling, bacony, fattening, juicy, beautiful,

With dribbling brown sauce is how I like it most.

Jack Radley (8)
Shelton Junior School

I'M A MOTORBIKE

I'm a motorbike, a racing motorbike
Zooming down the lane,
When on a racing track
I'm soaring there and back.

I'm a motorbike, a racing motorbike
Zooming down the street
I'm down Donnington Park
I'm there till it gets dark.

I'm a motorbike, a racing motorbike
Zooming round and round,
Went round a roundabout
Gone wandering about.

I'm a motorbike, a racing motorbike
Zooming down the road,
When I'm off very fast
People need a good blast.

Jake Nicholas (9)
Shelton Junior School

ADJECTIVES FOR BREAKFAST

Hot, fried, soft, buttery bacon.
Fried, hot, buttery, soft bacon.
Buttery, soft, hot, fried bacon.
Bacony, soft, hot, buttery, fry.
Soft, bacony, buttery, hot, fry.
Bacony, fried, soft, hot, butter.
Soft, fried, hot, buttery bacon.

With tomato sauce is how I like it most.

Matthew Lewis (8)
Shelton Junior School

AEROPLANE

I'm an aeroplane, I am a jumbo jet,
With my swooping wings,
I can swoop, I can sway,
Making clatter all day.

I'm an aeroplane, I am a jumbo jet,
With my thumping floor,
I can scare, I can bounce,
Until I make a pounce.

I'm an aeroplane, I am a jumbo jet,
Leaping in the sky,
I can leap, I can groan,
Till I make the earth moan.

I'm an aeroplane, I am a jumbo jet,
With my screechy wheels
I can screech, I can break
Making people awake.

I'm an aeroplane, I am a jumbo jet,
With my creaky roof,
I can creak, I can bash,
Making a big, big crash!

Gracia Colabufo (9)
Shelton Junior School

THE MINOTAUR

There once was a ferocious beast,
Who terrified all the Greeks,
Half man, half bull,
He was very cruel,
His name, The Minotaur.

His horns were sharp,
Like the tooth of a shark.
No man or thing
Would enter his labyrinth
And ever come out again!

Richard Hammond (9)
Shelton Junior School

I'M AN AEROPLANE

I'm an aeroplane, a modern air crew's plane,
With my metal wings
I can soar, I can swoop
Till I go round in loops.

I'm an aeroplane, a modern air crew's plane,
With my jet engine,
I can fly up like flies,
Till I'm high in the sky.

I'm an aeroplane, a modern air crew's plane,
With my metal wheels
I can screech, I can scrape
Till clouds are different shapes.

I'm an aeroplane, a modern air crew's plane,
With my new windows
People can see out
Without an awful doubt.

I'm an aeroplane, a modern air crew's plane,
If you want a ride
It won't be a delay
So please call me today.

Amy Swarbrook (9)
Shelton Junior School

STEAM TRAIN

I'm a train, an old steam train
With my smelly steam
I can huff, I can puff,
My steam comes out as fluff.

I'm a train, an old steam train
With my flashing lights,
I can dazzle once more
When we are near the shore.

I'm a train, an old steam train
With my rusty wheels
I am scraping the rails
Delivering the mail.

I'm a train, an old steam train
With clear windows,
People are looking through
Just like they always do.

I'm a train, an old steam train
With my creaky door,
It opens and closes
Letting passengers through.

Emma Scott (9)
Shelton Junior School

THE MONSTER UNDER THE BED

There's a monster under my bed,
He's green and hairy and very scary,
He has huge arms, anything he sees he harms,
His name is Gnasher because of his big teeth and giant claws.

There's a monster under my bed,
His eyes are brown and he wears a crown.
His hair is red and it pokes out the bed.
He has such big muscles
He could crush a human if he had half a chance.

Adam Holmes (10)
Shelton Junior School

THE MONSTER

The monster is green,
He is fierce and mean,
He eats rabbits,
He has habits,
The monster likes the Queen!

He sleeps in a cave,
Like a microwave,
He is 7ft tall
You cannot hear him call,
He can't wave.

Up the hill he goes,
Without any clothes!
He always stamps,
He never camps,
His voice always echoes.

Jamie Edmonds (10)
Shelton Junior School

THE SCHOOL JOURNEY

Here I go on my way,
Jingling dinner money,
Ready to pay.

Passing the houses and the shops,
Lost my dinner money,
I want to stop.

I see a bird in the sky,
Through the mud I carry on,
Now I really have to fly.

Round a bend,
The school appears,
My journey has come to an end.

David Todd (10)
Shelton Junior School

IMAGINE

I   magine a land where animals roam.
M   agical witches in the sky.
A   mazing cities behind walls.
G   reat palaces grand and gold.
I   nstruments playing all day long.
N   aughty dragons playing games.
E   very day there's an adventure.

Benjamin Stevenson (8)
Shelton Junior School

A SLOW BARGE

I'm a barge, a slow barge,
Too small for the sea,
I can float, I won't sink,
My driver needs to think.

I'm a barge, a slow barge
The sea is no place for me
I can smoke and use steam
Not as fast as a stream.

I'm a barge, a slow barge
With my whirling blade
I can rotate and take
People over the lake.

I'm a barge, a slow barge
With my good driver
I can move round and round
But not on the hard ground.

Greg Tatem (8)
Shelton Junior School

WHAT A MESS!

Chocolate down my clothes,
What a mess!
Toys everywhere,
Clean it up!
Bed's in a mess,
Where's my cover?
Mum's getting angry,
What a mess!

Gemma Stubley (9)
Shelton Junior School

My Sister's Room

M agazines on the floor,
Y o-yo on the bed.

S cissors on the shelf,
I nk pens in the toy box,
S tains on the walls,
T oys on the window sill,
E very shoe on the bed,
R evolting it is, I'm being honest,
S he doesn't care, so leave her to it.

R eindeer bag on the door,
O range peel under the bed,
O h! So here it is, my watch, I found it.
M ore mess on the landing too.

Kristian Thomas (9)
Shelton Junior School

My Mum

She's a leopard hunting for its food,
She's a cuckoo bird singing a beautiful song,
She's the smell of a rose bud waving in the sun,
A spicy meatball sweet and nice,
She's every colour of the rainbow,
She's the summer sun shining down on me,
She's a chair bouncing everywhere,
A car racing when she is mad,
A bubbling stream flowing down a mountain,
She's powerful music being heard everywhere.

That's my mum.

Jessica Mannion (10)
Shelton Junior School

MY BABY SISTER

M essy as can be
Y ip, yap all day.

B ottles everywhere,
A lways crying,
B aby's toys everywhere
Y ogurts all over the floor.

S illy and naughty every second,
I cky, sticky lollies everywhere
S ick all over you
T reats in the jar
E verything really smelly
R ather nice at times.

Samantha Weedon (9)
Shelton Junior School

THE FIRE BREATHING DRAGON

He came out in a puff of air,
When he roared he raised people's hair.

His scolding hot fire was as warm as the sun,
He scared everyone away, as well as the nun.

His belly rumbled and made the Earth shatter,
When he walked he made a big clatter.

He blazed out fire into the town,
It even reached the king's house and knocked off his crown.

Sammy Needham (9)
Shelton Junior School

PIGS

There was a young pig
Who put on a wig,
Her eyes shone bright
And said 'It fits just right.'
I love this mud
It feels good.
She went in her pen
And said 'What a good den.'

The sty was wide
But she just lied.
She eats lots of hay
On this very day.
The trough was metal
She was a little petal.
She goes to bed at night
And wakes back up in the light.

Kayleigh Waters (9)
Shelton Junior School

THE BEACH

The grey whipping sand.
Blue waves lapping on the shore.
The black breakwaters.
Boats sailing across the sea.
Sea lions diving about.

Louise Muggleton (10)
Shelton Junior School

MASSING LOSS

What is the meaning of life?
Why does matter exist?
Man is born, but deceased.
Man finds partner, finds wife.
Is there an end to this dotted rhythm of life?

Man has been dominant,
Man has also held back,
Will man's twisted memory
Ever lose its track?

The Earth is a massing loss,
Man is born to die.
For life is an extended glitch
Our maker will never lie!

Jonjo Beal (9)
Shelton Junior School

SEASONS

Spring is when the lambs are born
And blossom covers the trees.
Summer is when children play
In water up to their knees.
Autumn is when the conkers fall
And the trees will soon be bare.
Winter is when the nights are long
And Jack Frost is in the air.

Helen Swan (8)
South Darley CE Primary School

THE FOUR FEELINGS

Lonely:
Feeling small,
All alone,
Everyone has a pal,
All apart from,
Little me.

Anger:
I'm hot,
Get out of my way,
You're horrible,
Smelly.

Envy:
It's not fair,
The whole world's got one,
Except for me,
I want it too.

Happy:
It's great,
I have a mate,
Someone to play with.

Abigail Holmes (11)
South Darley CE Primary School

CROC

He likes zebras,
And reindeer for dinner,
And horse for tea.

Thomas Wheeler (10)
South Darley CE Primary School

THE FOUR SEASONS

The time of new life,
The time of love,
Birds are chirping,
High up above.

We are all joyful,
When holidays come,
Fun and laughter,
For everyone.

Friendly colours,
All around,
New fallen leaves,
Cover the ground.

The cool, white snow,
Brings good cheer,
All too soon,
It's New Year!

Aimee Hall (11)
South Darley CE Primary School